"Bill Coleman not only helps parents understand what breaks their hearts, he also shares wisdom to help in the process of mending them."

Tim Robbins, Counselor

"Bill Coleman, like his Lord, is close to the brokenhearted. This book is emotionally freeing and spiritually energizing. Readers will find healing and personal meaning as they put into practice the fresh ideas and clear choices that shine from these pages. They will also discover some ways to help others who are hurting."

Dr. Paul Welter

"Bill Coleman has done it again. Every book he writes reaches out to touch us where we are hurting."

Charlie W. Shedd
Author of *Letters to Karen*
and *Letters to Philip*

Parents *with* Broken Hearts

HELPING PARENTS OF PRODIGALS TO COPE

Parents *with* Broken Hearts

HELPING PARENTS OF PRODIGALS TO COPE

William L. Coleman

BMH Books
Winona Lake, Indiana
www.bmhbooks.com

Parents with Broken Hearts

© 1996 by William L. Coleman

Revised edition, 2007
© 2007 by William L. Coleman

Published by BMH Books
P.O. Box 544, Winona Lake, IN 46590

Printed in the United States of America

ISBN 978-0-88469-257-7

Typesetting: Rachel Benner

For current information about all releases from BMH Books, visit our web site: www.bmhbooks.com

Acknowledgments

Parents who hurt are usually willing to help other parents in pain. The parents I asked to share their experiences all said yes. They know how deep, mysterious, and agonizing loss can be.

I have changed the names and rearranged the events to protect everyone involved. The stories and quotes are accurate but slightly repackaged.

Whether a defiant young person separates himself or herself for a couple of weeks or for a decade, his or her parents are crushed like a reed. They are stunned and may have trouble regaining their strength.

The purpose of this book is to describe what goes on in troubled families and to offer hope for a good tomorrow. Hope comes in all sizes and doses, but it has to be taken regularly.

I want to note the contribution made by Compassionate Friends, a self-help organization that assists grieving families. These parents who have lost children in death helped me see the wider picture of loss and recovery.

On the professional level, I am indebted to my good friend Dr. Paul Welter of Kearney, Nebraska. His input gave me a great deal of insight, though he can hardly be responsible for the finished product.

It takes a brokenhearted parent to know a brokenhearted parent. I hope we will be able to reach out and help each other through this book.

Contents

The Lord is close to the brokenhearted
and saves those who are crushed in spirit.

Psalm 34:18

Chapter 1

It Could Never Happen

What parents would ever dream that their newborn baby, their bundle of joy, could possibly grow up to a life of rebellion, lawlessness, or even separation from them?

Sitting in the hospital nursery, new parents aren't thinking about calls from a school principal, beer cans strewn across the lawn, flashing police lights, or sleepless nights. Their thoughts aren't crowded with unwanted pregnancies, drugs in jean pockets, or surly friends waiting outside to whisk their child away. They can't imagine sitting in courtrooms, counselors' offices, or corridors of institutions and wondering where they went wrong.

Some parents may never face such dark and agonizing scenes, but many do. And their hearts break. They break while the disastrous behavior is going on, and often they remain broken for years, maybe decades. These parents are left hurt and bewildered over what happened and what might have caused their child's behavior.

How are parents supposed to feel? Should they feel guilty, resigned, angry, vengeful, depressed? Should they keep trying to help their child, even when he or she is thirty years old? Or should they simply try to forget about what has happened?

How can parents with broken hearts find hope, spirit, and healing? How can they accept what has happened and enjoy a fulfilling life?

Parents with broken hearts are much like the survivors of auto accidents or other tragedies.

- They wonder why it happened to them.
- They wonder who is to blame.
- They wonder if they can hope again.
- They worry about their other children or their grandchildren.
- They lose much of their zest for life.

Parents who fight the normal battles of adolescence fall into one category. They discipline, negotiate, argue, and struggle for change. They share the adrenaline and challenge of trying to steer a moving vessel, their youthful offspring. A great deal is written about how to help these beleaguered parents stay the course and prevail.

Parents with broken hearts, however, fall into a different category. For them, the day-to-day struggles may be over. Their child may have moved out, be married, have a child, be in jail, be an alcoholic, or be a drug user. He may blame his parents for everything, may need financial support, may not be able to keep a job, and could deny the faith he was taught as a child. Yet little help is available for these parents.

Brokenhearted parents could experience any or all of this or a number of other terrible disappointments. What makes these parents unique is that their child has passed adolescence. The young adult carries the results of misspent teen years, but how do parents live with those distorted and painful results?

Ron and Linda's daughter, Renee, for example, became pregnant when she was a senior in high school. She decided to keep the child and not marry the biological father. Naturally, there were many tear-drenched evenings for the family as they discussed what had happened and why.

After consulting friends and a counselor, Renee concluded that she got pregnant because her mother and father failed to teach her birth control, and her father was frequently away at work, Renee reasoned that the pregnancy was their fault. The counselor encouraged her to confront them with this charge. Today Renee is married to another man and has a second child. She gets together occasionally with her parents for social obligations, but they are not close.

"How do we deal with this?" Ron wondered aloud. "It's hard to get together for Christmas and Thanksgiving when you know she blames us for the mess she is in. She can't get a job because she has no education, and they're always broke. Are we supposed to help them financially because we didn't teach her birth control? Every visit is simply tension city."

Wherever the blame might belong, the question remains: How are the parents to go on with their lives? Are they destined to flog themselves forever over the accusation? Should they help support the children to make everyone feel better? Would family counseling reduce some of the resentment? Can they block the entire episode out of their minds and act as if nothing happened? Are they doomed to be brokenhearted for the rest of their lives?

Caught in the Aftermath

Connie's son Daniel is thirty-two years old and has been an alcoholic since he was a teen. He bums around at jobs from time to time, but employment is getting harder to find and more difficult for him to keep. "He lives only fifteen minutes from here." Connie pointed east. "He comes over every once in a while."

"It isn't that I blame myself. I'm well over that," Connie continued. "My problem is what do I do now? If I hadn't paid his rent, he would have been thrown out long ago. I won't let him move back here, but I can't simply abandon him. "It's kind of like a toothache, only much worse. The pain is daily, and it never goes away."

Does Connie have a continuing obligation to help her own flesh and blood? Can she donate money to feed the homeless while she neglects her son in his need?

Millions of parents are caught in the aftermath of disruptive child raising. Some parents divorce after their last child leaves home partly because they cannot sort out their feelings. One parent wants to remain involved and continue to help the errant adult child, while the other parent wants to let him or her free-fall and pay the consequences. They are also conflicted about what happened, who said what, and why other actions weren't taken. Psychologically and spiritually bruised, the exhausted parents don't have enough energy to maintain their marriage.

Spiritual Wounds

A large number of parents are affected spiritually by such experiences. They prayed for their children. They may have had them baptized or dedicated. Millions attempted some sort of spiritual training either at home, or in a place of worship, or both.

Afraid to ask aloud, they wonder, *Where was God when it all happened? Why didn't He step in to do something to stop our raging delinquent?* Any attempt to heal broken hearts must deal with the questions raised out of spiritual pain and disappointment.

The Bible gives hope for those of us who have been cut to our souls. God promised to be close to the brokenhearted. We will look extensively at this spiritual dimension later.

As we work through the process of healing, let us claim Psalm 34:18 as our strength. "The LORD is close to the broken-hearted and saves those who are crushed in spirit."

For those who have pursued spiritual answers and found them unsatisfying, we ask only that you hang on to this simple premise. In chapter 16 we will deal with the tough issues of faith that most of us encounter.

Asking Why?

These things weren't supposed to happen to us. We can understand why alcoholic parents, abusers, adulterers, prisoners, drug users, or absentee parents would have serious problems with their children. But why us?

Many of us were steady, dependable parents who provided for our families. We went camping, we went to ball games, we bought our children good shoes. Though far from perfect, we thought we supplied all the essential ingredients. We helped with homework, went to teacher-parent conferences, and poured praise on the little tykes.

Most of us educated ourselves through books and church seminars. We disciplined, set limits, grounded our children if necessary. It's hard to believe we failed parenting. Perhaps we didn't deserve an A, but surely we didn't deserve an F. When the final grade came in, however, there was a glaring F.

"I may not have won the Parenting Award," said Mary, "but surely I should get a certificate of merit. I was there. I worked at it. I gave of myself. But my daughter acted like I was Wanda the Witch. She still resents me."

"I don't feel totally innocent, and yet I can't bring myself to plead guilty. Every other day I waffle between the two; and frankly, it's a miserable place to be."

Some parents with broken hearts find the remainder of life a bitter pill to swallow. They sulk in depression over what they feel is their great failure. Even if they are close to their other children, the perceived loss of the one child is overwhelming.

There are other parents, however, who are able to take hold of the rest of their lives. They have found a measured amount of hope and healing. Maybe a crack will always exist in their hearts, but they have found the inner peace and outer activity to make life worthwhile. Yet, parents' heads may still swirl with questions as they try to sort out the problems they have encountered. Hope and healing are available for every parent who has suffered a broken heart. As each chapter unfolds, I pray that readers will be able to see the light in their particular situations.

Chapter 2

Not Alone

Fortunately my entire church board came to my support," explained a pastor whose son was now away in the Army. "My son did it all. He stole. He was thrown out of school. He got into trouble while on a trip with the church youth group. You name it; he did it.

"At first I was afraid the church would turn on me. I was already disappointed with myself. I didn't think they would want to keep a pastor who had a rebellious teenager, but they seemed to love us all the more."

His story isn't rare. Many solid Christian parents see their children choose the wide path toward destruction. This knowledge doesn't change the terrible facts, but it does make us realize how normal we are.

Brokenhearted parents are members of a large, diversified fraternity. Its membership includes some of the kindest, most dedicated, and diligent parents imaginable. All are stunned and bewildered at the courses their children selected.

Two such parents were evangelist Billy Sunday and his wife, "Ma" Sunday, who suffered the loss of their sons, George and Billy, Jr. George lived in California, where he followed his love for wine and women. He was fond of driving along Hollywood

Boulevard with women in his Lincoln convertible. While in his late thirties, George either fell or was pushed to death from a seventh-story window.

Billy Jr. also pursued wild living. After attending an all-night party, Billy drove into a telephone pole in Palm Springs, California, and died instantly.

Neither of these stories tells us anything about the home life of Mr. and Mrs. Sunday. Maybe they were the best of parents or maybe they were the worst. Most likely their parenting skills were somewhere in the middle, like most of us.

But what of the biblical admonition, "Train a child in the way he should go, and when he is old he will not turn from it" (Prov. 22:6)? Many parents are angry with God because of their misunderstanding of that verse. They feel as if God made a promise and then broke the contract. However, Proverbs 22:6 is not a cause and effect promise. Rather, it is an axiom or wise saying.

In other words, it usually happens that way, but there is no guarantee. It could be a guarantee only if God took away a child's will. All of us have the choice to be the kind of person we want to be no matter what our training.

Take a look at family patterns in the Bible, and you will quickly see the jagged edges.

King Hezekiah was a godly man, but his son Manasseh was evil. Late in life, Manasseh repented and served the Lord. When he died, his son Amon became king at the age of 22. Amon immediately returned to the evil his father Manasseh had followed. And the Bible says, "But unlike his father Manasseh, he did not humble himself before the LORD; Amon increased his guilt" (2 Chron. 33:23).

Where is the guarantee in that pattern? Every individual must decide if he or she will follow the Lord, and many choose not to follow Him. While rebellion and degeneracy have always been treated as tragedies, they are neither new nor unusual. Original sin was rebellion against a heavenly Father, and the practice still exists.

Acknowledging the Problem

How many young people today are rebellious? There is no way to gain an accurate count, but a few well-known figures will give us an idea.

Annually, this is what happens among teens:

- One million run away from home.
- Two million are arrested.
- One hundred thousand enter mental hospitals.
- One million become pregnant.
- Half a million give birth.

Even a casual observer would concede this list is only the tip of the iceberg. Millions of other teens are in trouble and never make the statistical list. Most parent/child conflicts seem to center on nonlegal matters.

These conflicts seldom appear on police records:

- Young adults who never call, write to, or visit their parents
- Teens who have told their parents they hate them
- Young adults who have rejected faith
- Young people who have become alcoholics
- Children who married abusive mates
- Young people who have stolen from their parents
- Children who have joined cults
- Adult children who live for drugs
- Young fathers who don't support their children
- Siblings who dislike each other
- Adult children who have been told that all their problems come from their parents
- Silent children who never express their frustrations.

This is only a sample list. Some parents have a combination of these circumstances, while others are in unique situations. All together, the number of parents and families affected is extremely high. As a father recently told me, "That parents have broken hearts may not be normal, but it certainly isn't abnormal."

It isn't popular to admit that we have trouble with our children. While I was speaking at a seminar in Canada, I asked the group: "How many of you have trouble with your children?" No hands were raised. I was disappointed but not shocked.

Out of frustration I said, "Well, I guess I'm the only one who has trouble with his teens." Immediately hands began to pop up all over the room. These parents had trouble, but they weren't going to admit it if I wasn't. Parents aren't likely to volunteer that kind of information if someone is going to judge or lecture them. They will, however, become involved if they find others with similar experiences.

Ask yourself this question: How long would it take to name six parents who are brokenhearted because of their children? Look at your neighborhood, your workplace, or your church. Most of us would need only five minutes to think of plenty who are in the same rocking boat.

Looking for Understanding

Hearing an academic specialist talk about parental pain may be helpful, but it is seldom enough. Most parents with broken hearts are looking for someone who understands how they feel.

Parents are looking for someone who:

- has spent more than one sleepless night
- has watched a dream fall apart
- feels betrayed by someone he or she loves
- has felt helpless in the face of needless waste
- has tried everything
- can't shake the feeling of bewilderment

- has wrestled with self-blame and self-doubt
- has done something stupid in a desperate attempt to make things right
- has begged God to change things.

These and other experiences make us members of the same club. We are the emotionally devastated who have tried to reconstruct our feelings and go on through life courageously.

Such wounded spirits exist all around us. Many are willing to help while at the same time looking for help themselves. Knowing that others share our pain is a benefit. Although that knowledge will never heal the wound, it is important to recognize that others have been wounded, too. Nothing that may have happened to us is entirely unique.

We are all members of the same human race, often members of the body of Christ, and yet we suffer from this same sense of loss and heartache. For many faithful parents it's like having hot coals poured on their heads.

David stands out as a prime example of a father whose son rebelled, broke his heart, and even tried to kill him. Absalom, King David's third son, hatched a revolution against his father, and incited the people to rise up to overthrow the king. Collecting a huge following, Absalom soon had himself anointed king. When his army met King David's in battle, the revolution was quashed and Absalom's army was defeated.

When Absalom fled on a mule, his flowing hair became entangled in an oak tree, leaving him dangling in space. Joab, David's general, moved to the spot and plunged three javelins into the helpless man's heart. Ten of Joab's armorbearers then finished killing Absalom.

When David heard the news of his errant son's death, he wailed, "O my son Absalom! My son, my son Absalom! If only I had died instead of you—O Absalom, my son, my son!" (2 Sam. 18:33).

David can understand. He was there. David understands every parent who has ever put his face in his hands and wept, "My son, my son" or "My daughter, my daughter."

Many parents have experienced and still grapple with problems surrounding their children. If we can learn from them, we are better able to face our situations with courage.

Chapter 3

Separation and Loss

Most children experience separation anxiety. They are afraid their parents will leave them at the babysitter's and never return. Adults have the same anxiety, fearing that the people they love will go away, reject them, and not return. Each loss in life is difficult when it involves someone we care about and someone who cares about us. The loss of a parent, a spouse, or a child is a terrible personal blow if there has been a loving, caring connection.

Parents who have lost a child through death, rejection, or imprisonment share feelings of terrible separation. The details of their situations may differ, but at the bottom of the losses is the misery of separation.

A father once told me, "People think I live in agony because my son is a bartender. I am afraid they miss the point. For the past fifteen years I have reached out my arms to my growing child only to have him reject me. He has kept his distance and remained a mysterious character. His job is of minimal importance to me. It is our separation that hurts me almost on a daily basis."

Losing the Dream

How did we picture our child's future as he or she grew up? Did we imagine a bright-eyed, energetic son dressed up for

13

some special recognition? Did we picture the evening when our daughter would introduce us to her awkward date?

And how did we picture our family in the future? Did we dream of the family sitting around a Thanksgiving Day table and laughing together late into the evening? Were we looking forward to playing with our grandchildren?

Something happened to shatter those dreams of a whole family. Death, absence, or trouble has left gaps in that family picture. Our hearts are broken—for the child, for the siblings, for the extended family, and most of all for ourselves.

"Incomplete" is the word that fits each of these situations: Todd was killed at sixteen; Emily moved away at seventeen; Richie went to prison at eighteen; Marcia ended her own life at nineteen; Karen is twenty and refuses to contact her parents; Lance is living the estranged life of an alcoholic. None of these scenarios is what the parents had in mind. The family picture, their child's life, and the parents' lives are all incomplete. And they might always be.

We don't know for sure what the young person was thinking. Most likely he or she had a different scenario in mind, too. What we *are* sure of is that the parents were thinking in another direction, which is why their hearts are shattered.

Brokenheartedness is something we cannot understand adequately until we have experienced it. Studies of robins with empty nests or monkeys with no one left to preen fall short in discussing personal loss. A parent with wrecked dreams feels as if he has just been kicked in the stomach. No one else can fully understand this feeling of loss.

Brokenhearted parents must learn from other brokenhearted parents. Professionals can add knowledge and point toward help, but only one who has "been there" understands. A parent cannot know what it feels like to throw his sixteen-year-old child out of the house unless he or she has done it. A father cannot understand what it is like to tell his daughter, "I don't care if you have no place to live" unless he has said it. Only a parent who has been there can appreciate the agony of staying awake all night wondering where his child is. Who else, except one who has done it, can understand the emotion of a parent who packs his child's things in boxes for the last time?

Almost everyone will have to deal with some form of serious separation and loss eventually, but those who are separated from their children endure a peculiar kind of agony. Even parents who have experienced loss cannot totally empathize with other parents. While some losses are similar, no two are identical. Each family has too many dynamics going on for any two losses to be exactly alike.

Here are a few types of losses:

- **Death of a child.** A life is gone from this earth. The child is omitted from all future pictures.
- **Death by suicide.** The child is removed by his own choice. The reasons leading to the decision to take one's life may be confusing and are certainly painful.
- **Confinement.** The child is in prison, a mental hospital, or other facility for an extended period of time. Confusion and guilt might overwhelm family members.
- **Moving away.** Living over a thousand miles away causes a sense of loss, although visiting the child as often as possible partially alleviates the pain.
- **Tentative rejection.** This person will contact his parents if they respond as he or she wants. The child might demand money, gifts, or acceptance of lifestyle, or use other manipulative approaches.
- **Living rejection.** A child tries to avoid his parents most of the time if not entirely. On the rare occasion they do get together, the child seems impatient, hostile, secretive, belligerent, or negative.

Several other losses are not included in our discussion. Runaways, kidnappings, and cult recruitment are all losses

15

with different shades of experience and pain. However, while every loss is different, they do have some similarities. If we love someone, we suffer when we lose that person regardless of what caused the loss. Voluntary and involuntary loss are two sides of the same coin, but both are difficult to rationalize.

There is a significant difference between those who have lost a child to death and those who have lost one to estrangement. Parents separated from their children by death can idealize their child's lost future. They can imagine that he or she would have been an upstanding, thoughtful, and kind person.

Among parents with estranged children, the feelings are different. They have lost their idealism. Their child's behavior reminds them that terms like "upright," "thoughtful," and "decent" may not now or ever apply to their child.

Many parents will admit privately that they wish their child lived in another town. They never know what might happen— an auto accident, imprisonment, a pregnancy, abuse, or anything else unpleasant could occur any day.

These parents don't want any more such surprises. They are tired of juggling their feelings. Worn-out, disillusioned, bewildered, and aching, they hope the problem will end.

Some also admit they might be relieved if their child died. No one can understand that feeling unless he or she has had it. Many brokenhearted parents look for closure. If they don't expect the situation to improve, they secretly long for an end to the pain.

Some parents picture a phone call from the police or a hospital. They may envision a few tear-filled minutes to say good-bye to their dying child. Their imagination takes them to a coffin, possibly a graveside, and to some form of finality. These parents know they will have to wrestle with the memories but no longer feel able to battle with the present.

Many parents have said to themselves, *I brought her into this world and I will take her out.* Don't be shocked that you may have thought that.

The cry is for closure. Parents want to be happy with their children, and they are not prepared to war with them continuously. Their child has become like an abscessed tooth. No longer able to bear the pain, they wish it could be extracted.

A few years ago a minister shot and killed his famous musician son. The son was believed to have led a drug-wracked lifestyle entirely opposite to what his father had hoped. When the son came home to celebrate a holiday, his father took a gun and assumed responsibility for his grown child's life. Unable to accept his son's value system, the father wrongfully took action against his child's behavior. While many parents think about drastic measures, fortunately, most are called back to their senses.

Parents need to understand why they are tempted with such thoughts. They don't want to see others hurt, and they are weary of being hurt themselves. The feelings are normal but unacceptable. Death is not an effective form of closure. Our consciences eventually kick in and remind us of that.

The Lost and the Losers

Separation frequently leads to spiritual awareness. Parents feel their faith being challenged. Some become stronger through the experience, and some become bitter. Others are simply bewildered. All of us need to be reminded that God is familiar with our circumstances. Throughout the situation, the Lord continues to love everyone involved, both the lost and the losers.

Jesus taught about God's compassion for the lost. In Luke 15 He illustrates that God is like a shepherd who leaves ninety-nine sheep to look for one that has gone astray. There can be no doubt that the Lord is looking for our child. Wherever he is and whatever the circumstances, God searches for him and invites him to come home. We find comfort in the fact that the Lord is in loving pursuit of the person we love. God feels the way we feel. Often God experiences the same sense of separation that parents do. His heart also breaks for the child who is lost. When the child comes home, God will rejoice with tears in His eyes.

Jesus Christ is also heartbroken over the brokenhearted. He journeyed to see Mary and Martha because their brother had died. The Bible tells us He comforted them in "the loss of their brother" (John 11:19). It was no mere token visit to the grave. We are told that Jesus wept over the separation of this brother from his sisters. Even though He knew they would soon be reunited, His heart was crushed under the grief.

God doesn't take sides in a family squabble, nor is He a neutral referee. The Lord weeps for both sides. Parent and child are both losers in a separation. God knows that and calls out in compassion to both. Like a bridge across the long gap, our heavenly Father reaches out and touches both of us at the same time.

Chapter 4

Why Children Hurt Parents

Kelsi's behavior was causing her mother to come unglued. The high school junior's use of pot, her all-night absences, and her refusal to have any conversation with her parents were more than her mother could handle.

Kelsi's father had explained the situation to her often. Her mother couldn't sleep, cried daily, and apparently had lost much of her will to go on. In light of her mother's deep love for Kelsi, shouldn't Kelsi change her lifestyle so her mother could find peace?

"Tell her to buck up," the normally tight-lipped Kelsi told her father. "She's a fool to worry about me. I can handle myself. Don't try to pin her problems on me."

This girl wasn't stupid. She could see that her mother and her father were suffering. In order to continue her behavior, Kelsi needed a logic that was not logical at all. She needed to wrap herself with lies to insulate herself from the truth.

Teenagers know they are hurting someone but often choose to ignore the pain they cause. This choice may not make sense to the adult reader, because the logic of youth is extremely immature.

When a young person abuses the people he or she loves, we become angry. The abuse doesn't make sense, but it doesn't have to make sense. As we search for reasons, we must be prepared to abandon logic, or our hunt will be futile. If a teenager on the rampage accepted responsibility for his actions, he would stop. The fact that he doesn't proves that he rejects responsibility. If his life were a dot-to-dot puzzle, the lines would not connect. It is not that he couldn't connect them; he chooses not to. For example: a young man steals the family car, hot-rods around, smashes the car into a tree, and totals it. His father and mother are angry, hurt, disappointed, and crushed. But the son thinks to himself, "What's their problem? They have insurance. Dad is financially loaded. They can get a car. I'm not hurt. What are they angry about? I'm the one who almost got killed." When he draws lines to the dots, they don't reach.

If the young person connected all the dots, he would have to change his behavior. Therefore, he denies that his behavior is related to the problem. He rejects cause and effect.

A young man came to meet me because his girlfriend was dumping him. He and another girl had had sex. "My girlfriend says she's hurt," he said defiantly. "Does she have any idea what my needs are? I was lonely, this girl was available, and I needed someone. Then my girlfriend gets all upset about it."

His dots all connect to himself. He can't draw the line across to reach his girlfriend. In his extreme immaturity, he refuses to take that step.

A child believes she causes everything that happens. She makes people smile, frown, appear, and disappear. Growing older, she learns that life is interactive and people affect each other. The rebellious teen doesn't like that stage of life and decides to drop the concept of responsibility. She prefers to think that she is not responsible for anyone else's feelings.

Self-Centered or Self-Reliant?

We sometimes assume that all teens are basically self-centered. That isn't true, of course. Millions of young people manage their lives and care for others at the same time. Some teens drown in their own needs, while others swim very well. Teens may have self-centered needs, especially as they discover themselves, but not all of them are blinded by it. Like adults, teens are self-centered in varying degrees.

The completely self-centered teen refuses to humble himself to care for others. He is in no condition to ask what his parents might need. "Need means me. Need doesn't mean parents. It's too much to think through."

Those are choices teens make for their own purposes. Each decides which way to go. Teens can't be expected to be fully sensitive to their parents' needs, but many are partially aware. In fact, some teens work hard not to hurt their parents. Others are entirely self-centered and self-confident.

It doesn't bother me," one teenager claimed as he faced his court appearance. "I can handle it. Just leave me alone." This teen had convinced himself of two things: 1) I don't hurt, and if I did, I could take care of it, and 2) I am invincible and can do anything.

That's basic adolescence. Anyone who works or lives with teens knows that is how they feel or pretend to feel. You have to admire their courage and tenacity. The problem is they transfer their beliefs to their parents. If a teen feels this way about himself, then his parents ought to feel that way about themselves too. A teen believes if she doesn't hurt, they shouldn't hurt. If she is indestructible, they should be indestructible.

Why does the teen believe that? Because it works best for her purpose. When told that her mother is falling apart, the daughter says, "Well, tell her not to."

It works for her, but it's good to let the young person know you hurt, because she needs that information. But don't be surprised if she rejects it and remains insensitive.

These feelings aren't restricted to rabble-rousers. Terri was fourteen when she became a Christian. She didn't think her parents were Christians, so her local church encouraged her to evangelize them.

First, they fortified her with a set of values. According to the church leaders, her parents were lost, didn't know anything, and needed to be rescued by their teen daughter. Terri, feeling invincible and above pain, was now also convinced she was superior to her parents. The church assured the young lady that she held the keys to heaven and hell in her hands.

Having a relationship soon became all but impossible for Terri and her parents. Their feelings were of zero significance to this teen. She had a higher calling. If they didn't surrender to her teaching, they would remain lost forever.

Any way of thinking that causes young people to ignore their parents' feelings sets up an explosive family situation. We should never encourage teenagers to think their parents' feelings are insignificant. Too often parents are needlessly hurt by teens who are pursuing excellent goals. Some forms of self-centeredness come from otherwise good causes.

Nowhere is the evidence more obvious than among divorced families. Young people seldom connect to the pain their divorcing parents are experiencing. Typically, teenagers are swallowed up by what the divorce will do to them. "Will we have less money, no car? What about college? I hope it doesn't interfere with the prom and other big events."

The teen figures his parents created the divorce, which is true. If the divorce hurts, they should call it off. It's that simple in his mind. He has no time or emotional energy to try to understand his parents' pain. There is too much pain in his own life for him to be sensitive to his parents' needs.

If a teen has trouble relating to parental pain surrounding divorce, there is little hope that he or she can relate to the pain of rebellion. The defiant youth would have to get himself together before he could feel for his parents. By definition, that is an oxymoron. It's like saying, "Why doesn't a rebellious, defiant, self-centered teen start caring about his parents' feelings?" The two emotions are at war with each other. If the teen cared about his parents' feelings, he would stop his irresponsible behavior.

Helping Parents Cope

Parents need to get a grip. In most cases, they can expect little help from their teen. They may never get any help from the teen, but there are several steps that could help.

Tell the teen.

Don't assume that the young person knows she has hurt you. Give her information. "It tears me up when you don't come home on time."

Take steps to change the problem.

Never imagine that your child will see your hurt and adjust his behavior. Though this could happen, it seldom does. Take action and be specific. Take car privileges away. Ground your child. Tell your son or daughter he or she can't go to the party. Don't be content to let the young person hurt you.

Don't pout.

Self-pity is not a good way to turn a young person around. "Bleeding-heart" parents accomplish very little in constructive behavior change. Declare your pain, rise above it, and get on with your life. Parents who pout and display self-pity become ugly figures who accomplish nothing.

Set other goals.

Go back to the bowling league. Join a Bible study group. Apply for a promotion at work. Rise above the pain and continue with your life.

"I thought about dropping my Sunday school class," explained a mother whose son was in jail for six months.

"I figured I had nothing to teach. Besides, what would the parents of my students say? But I'm glad I didn't. I know now that God uses people who are from imperfect families."

Don't expect anything different.

Cursing what you can't change will only make the pain worse. Don't let the hurt drive you into bitterness. A young person may take a decade or more to realize how much pain she has caused her parents. Maybe she will never realize it. Don't expect it to change until it does. Then you will be pleasantly surprised rather than continuously frustrated.

Two Dimensions to the Hurt

Parents should expect to be hurt. That's the price we pay for intimate and caring relationships, since pain is often part of love. But usually we are bewildered by two dimensions of the hurt we receive from our children. First, we don't understand why a young person has to go so far when he hurts us. And second, why does a child have to hurt his parents for so long, often way beyond the adolescent years?

Not every problem child goes to such extremes. He or she may have two to six years of fitful acting out and then calm down to normal life. Parents with broken hearts usually have a child who has gone to the outer limits. The youth's refusal to rein in his belligerent behavior is what drains the parents most.

That child fails to face the depth or the duration of the pain he has inflicted. Because of those two dimensions, the wounds are frequently difficult to heal.

Chapter 5

Letting Go

"I need three hundred bucks, Dad, and I need it today." A twenty-year-old daughter stood nervously, her voice cracking.

"Count me out this time," her father answered firmly.

"You don't understand! If I don't get three hundred dollars, I'm going to jail."

Her father looked her in the eye and told her sternly, "I will not give it to you."

How could a dad say such a harsh thing to his oldest daughter? When she was nine, they went to circuses, the zoo, and the park together. He bought her costume jewelry and barrettes for her hair.

It had been a long, twisted journey between those heart-covered barrettes and his refusal to cough up money: wrecked cars, stolen money, all-night drinking, running away, continuous lies, trips to court, and other painful escapades.

Like most stories, this one didn't take one leap straight from piano lessons to incarceration. Finally this wiser father decided to let his daughter go. Instead of propping her up again and watching her fall a few feet at a time, he removed his hand. He was resolved to let be whatever was going to be.

As parents we know we have to let go. Most of us, however, picture ourselves releasing our children under good conditions. We imagine letting go at a graduation ceremony, a wedding, a move to a good apartment, or a promising job. We envision the rites of passage as uplifting, hopeful, and progressive. We never dreamed we would let our beloved child go into the hands of the police, into a life of drugs, or to a life with a seedy crowd. We are shocked, disappointed, and hurt.

The product appears to be incomplete. Like a cabinet with wobbly doors, squeaky hinges, and a rough, uneven finish, it needs more work—a lot more work.

But the time comes when we have no choice. The product is leaving whether we think it's ready or not. The parent must say to himself, *This child is no longer in my hands.* Why the product has not been completed on time is no longer an issue. It is leaving regardless of its condition.

Not only are the parents' hearts broken, but so is their pride. Father and mother know they could have done better. They wanted to do better. But, forced to face reality, they swallow that pride and remove their dedicated hands and tools. They bite their lips, turn their faces to the wall, and bid the child Godspeed. They feel like the father of the prodigal son. And they are.

The Illusion of Control

Many of us thought we could protect our children, guide them, and turn them around if they needed it. When they were five years old, we could pick them up and carry them into the house. If they played in the mud, we could wash them off and close the gate. Parents have great powers of control over small children.

"I thought I had what it took," a father from Dallas wrote. "I love my son, and I was always home on weekends. I was a loving father who was in attendance. You would think that would do it. "If my son started to drift into trouble, I was there to set him straight. As with an electronic toy, I was there to make sure he didn't crash into anything. But somewhere I lost control."

There will come a time, sooner for some and later for others, when the controls will no longer work.

Recently a nutritionist told of her dream to control the eating habits of her children. They weren't going to become fast-food junkies if she had her way. Carefully, she measured food and dictated each ingredient that went into her children's diets. Finally, they arrived at school, toting perfect lunches complete with carrot sticks, organically raised wheat bread, and pure cranberry juice. Imagine the mother's chagrin when the teacher later told her how much the other students enjoyed her children's lunch selections. Every day at lunch hour, the nutritionist's children traded their finely balanced meals for the cupcakes and pizza slices provided by their friends.

There is no doubt that we do exercise some control, and well we should. But none of us should be surprised that our control is quite restricted in both time and scope. With each passing year, our children reach greater independence. We need to acknowledge and accept that independence whether or not we think they are ready for it.

Releasing Things that Separate Us

We have little hope of mending our parent/child relationships unless we are willing to release the things that keep us apart. Parents need to ask if anything is important enough to keep them apart from their child for decades, maybe forever.

"It isn't so much the money," insisted a middle-aged mother. "It's the principle. My daughter asked for a loan of a thousand dollars to make a down payment on a car. That was four years ago.

"She takes trips. She buys other things. But never once has she offered to repay the money. I feel like I've been cheated by my own daughter."

That is a common problem in families. The issue that must be faced is this: Should the mother try to teach her daughter a lesson by demanding the thousand dollars year after year? Or should she send her daughter a note forgiving the debt? By releasing the debt, will she have the hope of dealing with more important conflicts than dollars?

Forgiving the debt can be extended as an act of grace. At this stage in the relationship, an act of grace might be far more valuable than a demand for restitution. But many parents hold on tenaciously. The unkept promise, the missing ring, the unreturned tools, the stolen heirloom, the unrepented lie, the failure to call, the absence at the birthday party, or similar issues. Understandably, parents are reluctant to release the action against them.

We understand parents who refuse to budge. We also see the damage that is created by stubbornness. Healing is more likely to occur if we release the object. If we fight to regain it, we may push the shaken relationship even further away and make it more difficult to retrieve.

Andy wrecked the right side of the car and promised to fix it. He never did. Maybe it's time to write Andy a note and let the dent go. With or without a note, the mental and spiritual releasing of things, events, and promises is significant. The place to begin is within our own hearts and souls.

Humbling Ourselves

One of the greatest obstacles to letting our children go is pride. Whether we let them leave or toss them out, we must come to grips with our own failure. Why didn't it work? Where did we go wrong? Shouldn't we give it one more try? How are we going to tell the relatives? How can she survive on her own without us? It doesn't seem right to release this unfinished, barely civil young person to create havoc in the world.

A parent who lets go has to change his attitude from one of failure to one of acceptance. We are not saying, "Look at the terrible job I have done." Instead we recognize the fact that we were unable to guide our child in the way we wanted him or her to go. We tried, but it didn't work.

Humility is the apex of wisdom when it comes to letting go. Pride says we can still change this person. Humility is the beginning of progress and the hope for a better tomorrow. We cannot; therefore, we will not. That's when we let go.

The father of the prodigal son made that same choice. Why didn't he force his son to remain at the farm? Why didn't he make his son change? He could not; therefore, he did not.

Peter reminds us that God opposes our pride. However, the Lord shows grace to those who are humble (1 Peter 5:5). By acting with humility, we know we have come close to the heart of God.

Where are our children going? None of us can know for sure. They might be heading straight for the crack house, a house of ill repute, or a life of crime. Possibly, they will find a Christian friend, a loving pastor, or a mirror where they might take a good look at themselves. Letting go means letting go to anywhere.

The good news is that God will travel with our son or daughter. They won't be going alone. This is the true hope of every believing parent.

During that conversation, we tell God what we are doing. We are handing over our adult child to our heavenly Father. No longer able to hold her, train her, or protect her, we are accepting reality. We pray, "Please go with her where we cannot go. Please watch over the one we can no longer see. Let her know You love her as we love her." But we can no longer be there.

This is a gift that believers have. We rise up in pain and put our faith into practice. We've watched our child get on the bus or train, destination unknown. We've waved good-bye and asked the Great Conductor to keep an eye on him. Now we walk away and hope the next time we hear from him he'll have some good news.

What did we let go of?
- We let go of our dream.
- We let go of our control.
- We let go of our pride.
- We let go of our child.
- We let go of trying.
- We let go of parenting.

What didn't we let go of?
- We did not let go of our love.
- We did not let go of our faith.
- We did not let go of our pain.
- We did not entirely let go of our hope.
- We did not let go of our pleasant memories.

Only now are we able to step up and take on the challenge of the next stage in life. Something has to be done before any of us can move on. We have to let go. Soon we will begin to feel some relief and renewed energy. Our spirit may not snap back to where it once was, but at least our spirit will live again.

We have to let go.

Chapter 6

Sewing the Guilt Quilt

According to Viktor Frankl, each of us eventually faces the tragic triad. We will suffer from:

1. a fractured relationship
2. feelings of guilt
3. the death of a dream (e.g., a complete family).

Whether by a rebellious child, death, or other circumstances, most people will somehow wrestle with these stages in life. They aren't pleasant. We don't volunteer for them. However, they are normally a part of our load.

One of our best consultants on the subject is Job. He said, "Yet man is born to trouble as surely as sparks fly upward" (5:7).

Job also taught us, "Man born of woman is of a few days and full of trouble" (14:1). Some of us can be thankful that we have seen as little trouble as we have. But be certain, troubled relationships are the common experience.

In a previous chapter we talked about the fractured relationship and the death of a dream. The feelings of guilt, however, are tricky. If we accept that we have a conscience, guilt of one kind or another is inevitable. Guilty people feel guilt, but so do innocent people. It is hard to have a dynamic, meaningful relationship with another person without pangs of guilt at some time.

I should have been nicer; I could have been nicer; I would have been nicer, are all likely to run through our minds. While there are a few truly narcissistic individuals who have put their consciences to death, most of us do not fall into that pit. Listening to family members who have lost a child or sibling in death, we are immediately struck by how much guilt is evident— imaginary guilt and real guilt, guilt from actions taken as well as from actions not taken, parental guilt, sibling guilt, grandparent guilt, friend guilt, and several other varieties of guilt.

Because life is packed with trouble, life is packed with guilt. However, *feeling* guilty does not mean we *are* guilty. Suffering causes us to become confused. Too soon we begin to think we are guilty simply because we exist.

The Difference between Guilt and Guilty

When I take long walks, I sometimes surrender to a bout of energy and run. Gasping for breath, I promise myself never to do it again. A month or so later I forget and jog another short distance, much to my regret. Sporadically I run, but by no stretch of the imagination does that make me a runner any more than leaping makes me a triple jumper.

In the same sense, one error does not make a person guilty. If someone foolishly spends twenty dollars, that does not cause the family to file bankruptcy. The person bears guilt, but he is not responsible for what ultimately may happen.

This distinction is extremely important for parents with broken hearts. Because we were engaged in a relationship with our child, we have guilt. We may have done something wrong sometime, but those errors do not make us guilty of creating a wild child.

Not understanding that distinction drives many parents to paranoia. We add up each mistake and treat it as if it were the determining factor. We assume each error, accidental or deliberate, made this sad result.

It is true that some parents are major contributors to their child's erratic and delinquent behavior. Child abuse, total neglect, criminal activity, sexual abuse, and other offenses might play large roles in misdirecting a child. We would never argue that parents have no effect on their children. But even in some cases of severe parental abuse, the child has grown up to be a wonderful person.

Normal parental mistakes do not by themselves create a wild child. We have, no doubt, committed acts worthy of guilt along the way, but we are not guilty of producing this behavior. (If you, the reader, find this concept too hard to accept, you might want to speak to a minister or other counselor. Brokenhearted parents need to resolve this issue as best they can.)

No one should try to talk us out of feeling guilty when we are actually guilty. That isn't healthy for anyone. But we need to know that if we promised our child we would refinish her dresser and failed to do so, that failure does not make us guilty of creating an estranged and difficult teenager. The one does not produce the other.

Guilt and Grace

No matter what we think or rationalize, we may still feel guilty. Some of us are convinced we are guilty and do not want to be talked out of it. If we are unable to stop feeling guilty, the next best thing is to accept it. Give in. You are guilty. "Phew." Some of us will feel relieved.

If that doesn't give relief, it may help to ask, "How does a Christian handle guilt?" Turn to God and accept His boundless grace. We messed up either intentionally or unintentionally. We have erred, wronged, and sinned. We now have the opportunity to call on the generous grace of God and apply His love to our failings.

To do that, we must believe God has an endless supply of grace and He distributes it liberally. God loves me without regard to my previous or present behavior. Through Christ, God accepts me, forgives me, and welcomes me into His family.

"For it is by grace you have been saved, through faith—and this not from yourselves; it is the gift of God" (Eph. 2:8).

Since we may be unable to distinguish between false guilt and true guilt, there is a time to stop trying. The grace of God is able to cover both kinds. Give in. Ask God to make His grace sufficient for whatever is going on.

Accepting the Agents of Grace

Occasionally a delivery person comes to our house to drop off packages. I have always been receptive and pleasant to the man or woman who brings them. I like packages. Almost always they contain good things like books, fruit, clothing, or something else I enjoy. Not once have I run such persons off. I have never threatened their lives, thrown rocks at them, or otherwise attempted to maim them. Why should I? They bring me delightful gifts.

When a kind person attempts to bring us a sample of God's grace, why are we so quick to get the broom and chase him or her away? This friend, neighbor, or whoever came to deliver the grace of God is ready to do a work of grace in our lives. We make a mistake by slamming the door in his face.

If our spouse feels guilt, as his or her partner, we have the opportunity to be an agent of grace. By doing kind and thoughtful acts, and by saying loving things, we can deliver grace to our mate. The act or word of thoughtfulness does not have to be related to our parent/child relationship. A guilt-ridden person needs to experience grace so he or she can remember that grace still exists.

By seeing acts of grace in our own lives, we may well be rescued from an attitude of despair. The Bible says, "See to it that no one misses the grace of God and that no bitter root grows up to cause trouble and defile many" (Heb. 12:15).

Many parents with broken hearts stand dangerously close to the edge of bitterness. They are in danger of falling off the cliff. The acts of grace offered by friends and strangers alike can become the safety fence that keeps them from that gruesome fall.

It is unlikely that we will talk parents out of feeling guilty. Like muscles, the harder we pull, the tighter the muscles become. By surrounding the person with love, we may help the parent let go of the guilt.

Chapter 7

Envy and Self-Pity

This is a difficult time for us," a mother told me. "Our daughter's friends are graduating from college. We get invitations to their weddings or announcements about their babies. Each time we receive them, our hearts are torn all over again. We aren't even sure where our daughter is or when she might call."

Can any family with an estranged child escape the heartbreak of comparison? Probably not. We are bound to watch others live out the dreams we once had for our own child. That hurts.

Someday you will be standing in a store, and without warning, your eyes will lock on the young man who is bagging your groceries. As your eyes fill with tears, you will look away, hoping no one noticed. The sight of that young man will have triggered a memory. You remember when your son used to bag groceries. He had a haircut like this youth. Your son was working to save money to buy a car. Today he lives in Kentucky waiting for the statute of limitations to run out so he can come back to your state.

Even when your mind is active with healthy thoughts, the ghosts of your child's past will reach out and grab you. You will be feeding geese at the park with your granddaughter when it will hit you that this is the same place you fed geese with your own daughter. Then you will choke up.

There are some battles parents with broken hearts might always have to wage. They will struggle with memories, fight to stave off envy, and do hand-to-hand combat with self-pity. Each campaign is unique and may call for its own strategy. Whether we like it or not, each battle must be fought if we are to maintain our balance. To stop is to surrender, and none of us can afford to stop resisting.

The Envy Attack

Even under the best conditions we want what others have. In times of prolonged stress, however, we envy others all the more. Sometimes envy takes an even worse turn. Too often we are relieved to hear bad news about someone else's child. When we learn that the mayor's son got into trouble or the neighbor's daughter was suspended from school, our hearts might leap a bit. Not that we wish them ill. Instead, we are reassured that our family isn't so odd if other "good" homes have problems, too.

Comparing ourselves with others is a slippery business. On the one hand, we feel sickened to hear bad reports about others. Yet, that same news assures us that we really are part of the human race.

Parents need to keep envy in check, or we can easily slide into destructive behavior. When it comes to envy, the Bible gives us straight talk and instant wisdom.

- Put away all envy; it is a terrible way to live (1 Pet. 2:1).
- Love of others does not permit envy. We start to look at others perversely when we want what they have (1 Cor. 13:4).
- Envy is not a spiritual resource; it is a base desire (James 3:14).
- Envy distracts us from dealing with our own situation. Cain, instead of facing his own problems, killed his brother Abel because he envied him (1 John 3:12).

Few feelings will do more to sap our energy and sour the way we look at others than the demon envy. As Francis Bacon said, "Envy takes no holidays." It will haunt us every day if we give it free rein.

Eventually we will learn to rejoice in the good we hear about others and not in the evil. If we had the power to change people, we would set free every family trapped in the struggle over their estranged child.

Parents who feel hurt over their grown children are tempted to envy parents who have lost a child in death. They imagine that when a child dies, there is at least a sense of closure. With a rebellious child, parents are seldom able to rest. Tomorrow they might get a call that their son is going to prison, that their daughter is pregnant and doesn't know who the father is, or that their son has crashed his car and killed someone. There is fear of what tomorrow might bring.

They may not wish their child dead, but many admit it would bring a sense of relief. That feeling might seem strange to those who haven't experienced it, but remember that many parents with broken hearts have carried unbearable loads for up to thirty years or more.

When I have mentioned this phenomenon to parents who had lost their children to death, they replied that they understood. They realized people believe death is the end of something. But for them, death is not a sense of closure. They continue to live with the death of their child. Parents continue to weep, to remember, and to work out their feelings. Their child is gone, but the loss remains and so does the pain. While death may change the problems, it does not remove them. It merely brings a different set.

That is part of the problem of suffering. Our ordeal becomes so severe we think we would like to trade our pain for someone else's. As appealing as that sounds, we would still be suffering. And in the long run, all suffering must be dealt with; it cannot be bypassed.

Envy's Brother: Self-Pity

As a parent with a broken heart, don't you sometimes feel terribly sorry for yourself? That is a common emotion among parents who hurt. Envy and self-pity are two sides of the "Why me, Lord?" coin. Seldom do we have one without the other.

On a list of useless feelings, self-pity must be at the top. "Poor me" has no constructive value. It is a thumb-sucking retreat from reality. Though normal and perfectly understandable, it is without redeeming value.

Jonah collapsed in self-pity after his ordeal at Nineveh. His feelings were hurt so badly that he wanted to die. God briskly confronted the prophet about his attitude.

Self-pity leads to destructive behavior. We have been wronged, and we want it corrected, or we will throw a fit. If we throw a fit, someone might get hurt. That "someone" will likely be ourselves.

Those who look for ways to use their loss for something good must first rise up from the ash heap. Tomorrow cannot begin until we stop saying, "Poor me."

Self-pity is like an anchor. As long as it sits on the bottom of the lake, we will never be able to sail free. We are held rigidly to that one spot—the past. Only when we stop feeling sorry for ourselves will we be able to move on with productive, cheerful, and meaningful lives.

Fortunately, God has sent people who can help us through our toughest ordeals. Some of us meet regularly with such groups or individuals.

When two people with similar hurts first find each other, they think they have discovered a gold mine. But if all they do is agree about how tough life is, they have actually found an empty shaft.

Parents need to ask themselves a couple of serious questions: *Are our contacts helping us to move on to a meaningful tomorrow?* Or, *Are our contacts helping us rehearse the disappointments of yesterday?* The difference is vital.

We don't need people who continue to feed our self-pity. Ultimately, it is no comfort to sit around and say, "Aren't things awful?" Caring people help us move on.

Chapter 8

The Limits of Pain

Being estranged from your child is painful. Few words can adequately describe the feeling. Parents hurt deep down and the pain affects their attitudes, relationships, health, and a great deal more. Some parents feel the pain every day. Others experience it as a low-grade hurt that occasionally flares up with unbearable sharpness. While shopping at the mall a mother sees a young lady who appears to be her daughter's age, and suddenly the parent is overcome with grief.

Uncertain what might set off pain, brokenhearted parents remain uneasy and tend to distrust themselves. If someone merely mentions the word "family," a brokenhearted parent might wince. The word they believed would always bring them warmth, security, and happiness has now turned bittersweet.

Parental pain is highly individualized. People with backaches can point to the area that hurts. Those with headaches can locate what throbs. Parents with broken hearts feel pain in any number of locations and in a variety of ways. Some describe it in terms of headaches, sleepless nights, heartaches, stomach pain, or pain in their spirit or soul. For others, it hurts to celebrate holidays or even to hold a grandchild. A few hate to attend weddings, visit college campuses, go to family seminars, or watch family themes on television.

This pain is real, not imagined. Parental pain is serious, and it needs to be handled as any other form of genuine suffering. Every parent with an estranged child should be free to express and accept the reality of the loss.

Questions Brokenhearted Parents Ask

How long will the pain last?

The time chart of parental pain is totally unpredictable. The pain will last somewhere between two weeks and a lifetime. Some parents have gone to war with their child for a year or two and emerged as close friends and relatives. Others go to their graves bitter, disappointed, and lonely. There is no normal or abnormal length of parental pain.

Almost anything is possible. Parents who thought they would never be hostile toward their child have spent decades in hostility. Others who feared they would never be close to their child again have lived to fish together on the banks of the Wabash or sit side by side in the same pew.

Parental pain can be readily diagnosed, but it can almost never be accurately predicted. That's part of why it is so difficult to deal with.

What if the pain never goes away?

We are reminded of Paul's prayer that the "thorn" be removed from his flesh (2 Cor. 12:7-9). The thorn was not dislodged, but the Lord told Paul how to cope with the affliction. If the parental affliction is not corrected today, tomorrow, or indeed ever, how are we to live with pain?

Once we have resolved that this condition may be long-term, we are ready to look for the best way to live with our situation. Fortunately, there are solutions to this problem.

People all around us live with pain on a daily basis. Some have trouble tying their shoes or standing up straight. Some feel exhausted most of the time or take pills to make it through the day. Some carry splitting headaches to the office and smile when they want to cry. Suffering is part of the human condition, but many people who suffer rise up not only to face the day but to conquer it.

I recall hearing a speaker who reported that he suffers from back pain. He hurts every day. After two surgeries, he has found little relief, and the medical profession offers him no ultimate solution. There is no reason for this gentleman to believe the pain will ever go away. His condition has continued unabated for thirty years. The speaker said that persistent, long-term pain would change us. Remaining the same is not an option. People who want to go back and become their old selves again are wasting their time in dreamland.

Chronic pain forces people onto a new road. The good news is that the sufferer has the power to choose *which* new road. Some select the low road and follow the route to bitterness and dismay. Others change gears and take the high road to strength and fulfillment. The choice is up to the individual.

Paul's thorn in the flesh presented the apostle with a decision. Would he take the high road or the low? The Lord promised Paul that he would find God's grace sufficient in his chronic disappointment, but he had to choose to take the Lord's high road.

What if I can't change the situation?

We have the power to change some things, but other things we cannot change. In most cases, we are unable to alter our child's attitude. Therefore, we have to come to a couple of mature, healthy realizations. First, we cannot change our suffering. But second, we *can* change our reaction to it.

How does the continued pain of an estranged or lost child affect us? Does it:

- Make us feel like failures?
- Make us afraid to trust?
- Make us feel useless?
- Make us cheerless?
- Make us lonely?
- Make us feel ashamed?
- Make us feel confused?
- Make us brokenhearted?
- Make us feel like quitting?
- Make us morbidly introspective?
- Make us want to leave our family?
- Make us jittery and irritable?
- Make us blame each other?
- Make us depressed?
- Make our faith weak?
- Make our body hurt?
- Make us listless?
- Make us reclusive?
- Make us lose sleep?
- Make us sad?
- Make us angry and bitter?

If we have these or other reactions to our predicament, there is great news. Everything on that list is curable. There is not one thing on the list that cannot be improved. The only part that we may not be able to fix is the loss itself.

Compare that to some of the things we tell ourselves that are *not* true.

- "I can never forgive him." That's not true.
- "I can never trust again." That's not true.
- "I can't get involved." That's not true.
- "I can't believe in the Lord." That's not true.

People with chronic suffering can do all these things. They simply can't get rid of the pain. Consequently, we must choose the high road and rise above the suffering.

What we can't do is rectify the loss. We can, however, get a firm hold on much of the fallout.

The Limits of Suffering

When her daughter left home at seventeen to move in with a boyfriend, Joyce all but quit living. She avoided her friends. Previously she had enjoyed painting, but now she could no longer bring herself to pick up a brush. Sapped of energy, Joyce could not bear the thought of taking pleasure in anything. She did what many of us are prone to do. Joyce allowed the river of suffering to overflow its banks and flood her entire life.

Suffering can rage and flow, but it has certain limits. Pain is not omnipresent or all-powerful. Suffering can steal our comfort, but it has no right to wreck our marriages. Pain can restrict the use of our back or our limbs, but it cannot stop us from encouraging others. Suffering is by nature limited in scope unless we allow it to leap its banks and hurt every part of our lives.

Smart parents know their child's behavior can be potent and destructive. But there are limits to that hurt if parents keep the other parts of their lives going. If a parent failed to take an examination to become an insurance agent because his son was getting into trouble, that may or may not be the son's fault. A son's scope of destruction is usually limited. The father may have *felt* as if he couldn't take the examination while the trouble existed. In fact, he might have been able to take the test and pass it well.

Never give suffering more than its due. That hungry lion will eat everything it possibly can. But never throw it extra meat. Rebellious children should never be allowed to ruin their parents' romance. They should never be permitted to call a halt to normal family living. Protect your family as much as possible.

"I thought about resigning," Todd said with a sorrowful look. "Here I was, president of the church board, and my youngest son was the terror of the town. It was all I could do to face the board or lead the congregation. I figured they must be thinking,

'Who does this big hypocrite think he's fooling?' I'm glad I didn't quit, but I wrote my resignation more than once."

Todd's pain was roaring out of its banks. Fortunately, he decided to stop it before his suffering was permitted to flood the entire valley. Instead of becoming the father with a broken heart who resigned as chairman, he became the father with a broken heart who continued to lead the church. He accepted the limits of pain and charged ahead courageously.

The son of the governor of a Midwestern state repeatedly got into trouble. As the child of a famous person, his problems usually got big treatment in the newspapers. According to the papers, this young man was involved in an auto accident in which an older couple was killed. He was arrested for intoxication, was charged with using an altered driver's license to purchase beer, had his license suspended, and was charged with illegal possession.

We don't know if the son was guilty of all of these charges or not. We do know that the father continued to run for governor and was reelected. Maybe the governor recognized the limits of pain. Whatever his son's difficulties, the father did not stop living.

Pain will rip out whatever it can and destroy it. But smart parents will not let suffering take their spirit.

Chapter 9

The Wheel of Emotions

"How should I feel?" That's the cry of frustrated parents. Their neat little nest is being kicked apart—twigs, feathers, and grass are flying. How is a loving parent supposed to feel when the nest is being torn to pieces?

It's as if the parent is saying, "Help me; I have no experience at this. Tell me how to feel, and I will do my best. Am I supposed to be angry, loving, hopeful, afraid, confident, cheerful, controlled, violent, or what?"

Imagine a sailor whose boat is on fire. Does he fight the fire, collect his valuables, scurry to his passengers' aid, send a message for help, or simply jump overboard? He would do the right thing if he knew exactly what that was.

A parent under pressure doesn't know how to react. Does he punish, forgive, plead, smile, frown, cry, pray, or become cold as ice? Eventually, he will probably do all of them. He only wishes he knew which was appropriate at which time.

This book can't tell you how to feel. There are no illegitimate, illegal, or immoral feelings. The best feelings are the honest ones. If you hate your kid, that is honest; you hate your kid. No one should tell you that you don't. If you adore your kid, that is honest too.

49

Our task will be to help you see where your emotions are. You might then ask where you *want* your emotions to be, by the grace of God. Smart people try to take charge of their feelings. Their goal is not to mask and hide them. Rather, they might say, "I am filled with self-pity, and I must stop this destructive behavior." That's taking charge. We will need the enabling of the Holy Spirit, but emotional control is possible.

The Wheel of Emotions

Everyone's story is different. We can't say, "I know exactly how you feel." As much as we would like to say that, it simply isn't true. If we want to know how someone feels, we need first to ask him and then to listen to him. It is a great sin to shut off a person by pretending to know his emotions.

The wheel of emotions may help the reader find where he or she presently is. From there, the parent can ask where he or she might *like* to be and then work to get to that place.

Some parents with broken hearts may not complete the cycle. That's why I call it a wheel. The wheel might never go all the way around.

Briefly, let's identify each feeling and see if it matches our experience.

Fear

Our child begins to break away from our family and reject our values. Though this rebellion usually begins in the teen years, it sometimes begins at eleven years of age or lower. As the defiance increases in frequency and severity, parents' fears begin to mount. In the early stages they were bewildered, but now they are afraid.

What is happening? How can I stop it? Is our caring family about to fall apart? Are we losing control? Is this simply a phase? Should we get help?

A large part of our fear is the fear of abandonment. Someone we love is pulling away, and leaving, but not under good circumstances. That frightens us.

Most parents don't remain at the first level. It's too painful to live for years in continuous fear. The situation either gets better or worse, or at least the parents perceive it that way.

Despair

The situation isn't getting better. She stays out later; her attitude is worsening; this is the second time the police have stopped her; she is drinking more frequently. The problem cannot be ignored or tolerated.

We are driven to despair. But despair has benefits. It will force the parents to do something. Let's take the family on a vacation; let's get counseling; let's move to another school; let's start checking her homework.

Let's do something to turn this thing around. Like the sailor with a sinking boat, we must do something. Inactivity will surely lead to the loss of the vessel.

Things often must get worse before they can get better. Only when the situation becomes terrible are we likely to take action to make something happen.

Apathy

In the movies, people don't reach the stage of apathy. The celluloid parent usually wakes up, finds help, and at last is seen fly-fishing somewhere in Montana with his grown child. That's why we love movies.

My guess is that most people who read this book are hanging somewhere between despair and apathy. Tired of trying, they are about to give up or already have. Some are looking for permission to be apathetic.

Apathy means, "I don't care. I don't particularly love my son, nor do I hate him. I tried feeling both ways and neither helped. I don't want to care anymore." That is lifeless, dull, resigned, stoic, unmotivated apathy.

We become apathetic in hopes of protecting ourselves from suffering. It's an understandable, natural defense. We don't want to hurt any more. Because it hurts to feel, we refuse to feel.

Apathy is not an attempt to correct the rebellious child. It is an act of desperation to preserve *ourselves*.

Love and Acceptance

If our child continues to abuse alcohol, is an irresponsible parent, or goes to jail, can we love and accept him? This is a tall hill to climb. The question is: If my son never becomes lovely by my standard, can I love him anyway?

Many of us remain in apathy because it would be too painful to take an alternative. We don't want to go back to the suffering we had when we tried to change our child. But neither do we want to move on to love and accept the estranged child who may never change. Consequently, we remain isolated on the island of apathy.

Some day we might take another look at our child. He may not be any different, but we will see him through eyes of acceptance. And we will say to ourselves, "I love him anyway."

Parents can be helped by seeing the grace of God through another person's life. We might feel someone's love toward us when *we* are unlovely. It may take an overwhelming act of love before we are able to lower our guard and love our defiant child. Fortunately, this can and does happen in many families.

Some say we must love and accept our children exactly as they are. In truth, we don't have to. But if we fail to love and accept, the alternatives are distressing. Our children will find it difficult to call, write, or return to visit if we cannot love and accept them. Think of how painful it is to contact people who dislike you.

The runaway, move-away, stay-away child is unlikely to hurry home to parents who are filled with fear, despair, or apathy. Parents have to stop trying to change their rebellious child by lecturing or judging his behavior. Parents who do that are still in despair.

Some parents still live somewhere in the first three stages of the wheel of emotion. They might dwell in the cracks neither quite here nor there. But they have the power to move if they choose to. Otherwise their unwillingness to improve will injure everyone involved.

The important thing is to evaluate where we are and where we would like to be. Then we can ask God specifically what we can do to change the situation. The Lord is unlikely to change our feelings or attitudes. God seems to leave our will up to us. But if we decide to make the move, God is more than willing to help.

Parents sometimes dig in their heels and refuse to move. They cannot bring themselves to accept their child's lifestyle. But as long as they fight over lifestyle, love and acceptance will not happen.

Don't be surprised if the wheel of emotions moves back and forth. Some parents get all the way to love and acceptance, only to slip back to apathy. Their love and acceptance runs thin, his or her behavior worsens, and the wheel goes into reverse. Occasionally apathy drops back into despair, and we try to change our child again.

Expect the wheel to remain mobile. Seldom does it lock into position. But if it does slide back, it can move forward again. Love and acceptance are still the reasonable emotional goals.

Where Does Anger Fit In?

"I've been angry with my daughter for the past five years," a father told me. "I can barely talk to her in a civil tone. How in the world can I deal with this steamy anger?"

There is good news for this man if he is willing to accept it. Anger is not at the heart of his problem. This is a cosmetic, superficial emotion. The Bible treats anger like a mask that we can rip off anytime we want which is why we are told not to let the sun go down on our anger. When the sun sets, tear off the mask of anger. Keeping it on is not helpful.

Not that parents don't have cause to be angry. Your son lied, took some cash, and wrecked your car. You don't *have* to feel angry, but it's all right if you do. If a child has been in fifteen years of hell-raising, you have had plenty of opportunities to get angry.

But we have no reason to *stay* angry. Anger should be a brush fire, not a forest fire. Parents are wise if they express their anger verbally when it happens and then put it aside. If we are still angry over the ten-year-old phone bill, we have allowed anger to become destructive.

Some of us treat anger as if it were a teddy bear. We hold it, stroke it, and cuddle the furry critter every night. Possibly we have learned to love the anger bear and are afraid to give it up. The choice is clear. Do we prize our anger more than we prize a relationship with our child?

We aren't monsters because we become angry. Loss and brokenness are normally accompanied by anger. We have lost something that broke our hearts. Anger can be a healthy expression.

It's much like adrenaline. When fear strikes, our adrenaline pumps rapidly, permitting us to respond to the threat. For a short time we are stronger and faster. But when the danger subsides, we want our adrenaline to retreat to its previous level. So it is with anger.

Grieving parents may have a large array of emotions. Most are valuable at the proper time and at the proper level. Smart parents do not permit their emotions to run amok. They make a wise decision when they grab the reins and gain control.

Parents' anger rarely causes children to choose good lifestyles. Few young people will change their behavior out of fear.

"For man's anger does not bring about the righteous life that God desires" (James 1:20).

The best emotions are the ones we make work for us. Anger ceases to work for us if it is out of control or lasts too long.

Chapter 10

Secrets of Imperfect Families

When I was growing up, I admired a family I knew in Washington, D.C. The family members functioned well, were generally cheerful, and seemed to care for one another.

One day I took pen in hand and began to make notes about the unit I idolized:

- Dad has a sister who is a forty-year-old alcoholic and who seldom has a job.
- Mother has a parent who has been in and out of several mental institutions.
- Mother has a brother who was dishonorably discharged from military service.

Nothing they had experienced disqualified this family as a great example. Like others, this family is normal and has problems. They have situations to deal with that they handle in a reasonable fashion.

Why can't we all have a good family like this one? Most likely we will. We will have a child who will run away, two relatives who will divorce, a brother who will get cancer, an uncle who will be hooked on drugs, and a cousin who will go bankrupt. Generally speaking, this is life.

When such situations occur, we need to know we are normal. Rebellion, disgrace, disappointment, loss, failure, betrayal, anger, and even madness are part of the human condition. We can expect some or even all of these agonies to afflict our families.

Even the church family that we admire so much is not immune from these woes. Some of us will have more affliction and others less. The trowel of grief does not spread evenly, but all of us will receive a heavy share.

It is not our job to see how many families are worse off than we are. None of us should seek comfort in the knowledge that the Jones family has one more bank robber than our family has.

Our child's behavior will usually be consistent with the history of our family tree. Our genealogies are dotted with irregular and outrageous acts. Our problems are often similar to those of our own clan and other families.

"For all of the calamity that my son created, I must admit it was not unlike that of his immediate ancestors. Maybe none of our relatives went to these extremes, but neither is his behavior entirely foreign," a father shared.

"On my side of the family there are many social renegades who were forced to leave town under less than ideal conditions. And on my wife's side it was quite a bit worse. When it comes right down to it, we shouldn't be totally shocked. Disappointed, but not shocked."

The fact that others have gone through similar situations may be of little comfort, but let's take that small comfort, nevertheless. It proves that we are not "different." Normal, everyday, sane people with caring relatives crash into brick walls from time to time. We are people wrestling with common problems, experiencing common disasters *and* common successes.

We must recognize that commonality. To believe otherwise is unrealistic. Our ability to cope is tied to our willingness to say we are normal people who have had a tragedy enter our lives.

We are all torn by similar situations, although not identical. The Bible confirms our commonality: "No temptation has seized you except what is common to man. And God is faithful; he will not let you be tempted beyond what you can bear" (1 Cor. 10:13).

What bombards my family bombards your family. The temptations may come in different sizes, colors, textures, and at different prices, but they assault all of us.

Keeping Secrets

What are the secrets in the corners of our homes and family trees? Usually we have three kinds of secrets hovering ghostlike from our past:

- Secrets that aren't worth mentioning.
- Secrets we have forgotten.
- Secrets we guard.

Secrets aren't always bad or sinister. Sometimes secrets are pleasant memories that we savor. Other secrets, however, can be incidents we are trying to conceal, hoping others will not find out.

When I was in high school, I dropped out for an entire year. I came home one day at age fifteen and told my father I would not go back. A year later I walked back through the front door of Eastern High School to continue my academic life struggles.

My children will learn of this for the first time if they read this book. Why haven't I told them before? Until recently, I had forgotten about the grief I must have caused my father at that time. When my children were facing difficult times, I never thought to bring up that tidbit from my past.

If we look into our past, even our recent past, we are likely to remember a number of secrets. We may have told our family members a few. A couple of arrests or embarrassments we might hold solely for our own amusement.

Many women have had abortions but have never told their families. Some parents were previously married for six months way back when but have never mentioned it. Some mothers were abused as children. A cousin took her own life. A grandfather was severely depressed. One branch of the family had four children with three different fathers.

The value of taking a look at those secrets, maybe even sharing them, is that they give us perspective. Our family's history is not spotless, and we may find strength by accepting that fact.

When we listen to stories of the rural Midwest, we might think all of our ancestors traveled here as pioneers, each carrying a wagonload of seed and a Bible, and doing honest labor. It makes you wonder who is related to the drunks, criminals, and madmen who came this way at the same time.

Secrets have such a powerful hold on us that their weight is best measured when they are lifted. We don't appreciate how burdensome a sack is until someone lifts it from us. The same is true if we can admit the chinks in our family armor.

When we are able to share some secrets with our family or with others who care, we feel a sense of relief. Maybe we need only admit them to ourselves. Maybe we need to share them with our family so others can benefit from this information. They could be the secrets that our family needs to know to give them a balanced perspective and to help them see more clearly what is going on today.

The Myth of Perfection

It is a myth to believe there is a formula available that could lead to a perfect family. Though all of us may accept the fact that there are no perfect families, many still believe the formula exists.

We are deluged with "seven steps to a responsible child," "eight steps to a close family," "six steps to give our child self-esteem," or "five steps to obedient children." Such formulas, however, raise unrealistic expectations. They entice parents to take the steps to produce a certain type of child. Followed diligently, we are told, these steps will lead to a perfect family.

In reality they are traps. The formulas promise a perfect family, but we try the steps and our family is less than perfect. What went wrong? We conclude that the problem must be us. We tried the five steps, and our child didn't become obedient; therefore, we must have done something wrong.

Formulas on how to raise families ensnare us and result in gigantic guilt trips. That's the downside of putting so much emphasis on family. We idealize it, and when the ideal is not reached, we consider ourselves failures.

The *myth* of the perfect family exists, but the *reality* of the perfect family exists nowhere.

The Christian Crunch

For hundreds of years, Christian families have felt the pressure to look good. A solid, intact, even compliant family was considered a sign of faithfulness and spirituality. Families felt a need to make a happy appearance, even if the domestic unit was flaking away at the edges.

No one felt the pressure more than the pastor and the deacons. Disobedient or rebellious children were a disgrace to anyone holding office in the church. Today we feel sorry for the poor souls who fought so hard to hide their disruptive children.

Today there is more transparency. Congregations are far more willing to accept a minister with a wild teenager. Pastors are more likely to discuss their problems with individuals, board members, and even entire congregations.

The idea of the perfect family dies hard, but in many places it is now acknowledged as a myth. We applaud healthy families, but now we also accept all kinds. If a son rejects his family values or the Christian faith, fellow Christians are less likely to condemn the family. We know it happens, perhaps too frequently.

There are sad exceptions. A pastor in Wisconsin was recently dismissed from a church mainly because of his son's behavior. The boy's drinking, girl-chasing, fighting, and reckless driving became too much of an embarrassment to the congregation. Some of the teenager's conduct directly involved the young people at church.

The pastor was a faithful father. The son was a rebellious teen. Unfortunately, the entire family had to suffer because of the boy's refusal to comply, and it cost a good pastor his ministry.

Another nasty little secret is now out in the church too: Christian families don't always produce Christian children. And sometimes they produce Christian children who live horrendous lives. Seldom do we brag that Christian families are better than non-Christian families. Because so much depends on the individuals, we cannot make that wild claim.

More and more the Christian church is becoming a support group for imperfect families. Christian parents tell prayer groups their daughter is hanging around with the wrong crowd. Fathers tell support groups their son has a drinking problem or has been arrested.

The veil is lifting, and we see each other as fellow travelers in a dangerous world. This is the beginning of acceptance.

Accepting Our Imperfect Family

A few simple steps might help any family suffering from severe stress. Try to accept the following facts.

- My family is not perfect.
- My ancestry has never been perfect.

- Imperfect families are normal.
- I can live with an imperfect family.
- Many will accept my imperfect family.
- A few people will not accept my imperfect family.
- Since I am not perfect and since my spouse is not perfect, I have no reason to expect a perfect family.
- My imperfect family helps me accept other imperfect families.
- I must stop feeling sorry for myself.
- I have gained strength from my imperfect family.
- I should concentrate on my family's strengths and stop brooding over its weaknesses.
- Being a Christian does not guarantee I'll have a perfect family.

It's just a list, and it contains no magic powers. But if its elements are rehearsed and followed, they have the potential to change our outlook on our families.

We are in danger of putting family on a pedestal and worshiping this unit. Families are extremely important, but they are not everything. When families become everything, we are ill equipped for setbacks.

If our families are wounded, dysfunctional, or in disarray, life can go on. In fact, it can go on quite well. If we don't believe that, we lose the will to live when our son joins a cult or our daughter is on drugs. Those are terrible, terrible calamities, but life will go on for those who see life in a broader picture.

God gives us a wide array of reasons to stay involved in life. An imperfect family is never enough reason to give up and hate living.

Chapter 11

Birthdays and Holidays

"I think apple pie must be the hardest," a mother told me. "That was always his favorite. Every Christmas I made sure there was an apple pie because it made Derek so happy.

"Now it's too painful. I don't know if he will show up or not. I'd hate to have Derek come, and have no pie. And yet if I bake it and he doesn't show up, I will feel sad because the pie just sort of screams out at me."

Birthdays, Christmas, Thanksgiving, Mother's Day, Father's Day, anniversaries, and other special occasions can be miserable experiences for families suffering loss and separation. We look at those times as family gatherings. Now they are reminders that we are *not* a whole family.

It is one thing to have a daughter in Boston who can't be there for the holidays, but it is quite another to have a son across town who refuses to come. And having a deceased daughter whose picture hangs on the wall is completely different from both.

Families tend to fall into two categories. Some try to keep the traditions alive. Others look for new traditions and move ahead. The most satisfying holidays may be the ones where a few traditions are kept, but many new ones are added.

65

Changing the Routine

The goal is not to forget the person. His not being with you doesn't mean he never existed. It's unwise to try to erase him from your mind. That's toying with the facts.

A far better solution would be to keep at least one tradition that was special to this person. He loved spareribs, so you have spareribs at one meal, though maybe only as a side dish. He enjoyed opening presents before breakfast, so keep that practice and say why. Mention the person, if only once. Many complications arise when a family refuses or neglects to mention an estranged member. There is a reasonable middle ground where we acknowledge a loved one without dwelling on him. In the long run, the pain will be less if we can say his name in a balanced, civil tone.

Create new traditions so the family does not become fixed on sad regrets. If a family tries to freeze itself in the year when she was twelve, they take the chance of being locked in the past.

Acknowledge the person you love but can't have, at least for now. Then move on to be involved with the family members you can presently enjoy.

Extending Invitations

When relationships are seriously strained, misunderstandings regularly arise. Is she invited or isn't she? Is the family mad at her? Would they rather she didn't come?

Make it plain. Let her know she is invited. Be warm and sincere. Don't beg. Don't manipulate. Don't bribe. Be direct and friendly.

"We are having Christmas dinner Thursday night at eight. We would love to have you here, and bring your boyfriend with you."

Afterward make double plans. What will you do if they show up? What will you do if they don't? Keep it simple. You may hate the uncertainty of making double plans, but what else can you do? We can't have everything neat and cuddly; consequently, we are willing to accept some things in bits and pieces.

Buy her a present or put her name in the pool when you draw names. Every family member knows that disappointments might lie ahead, but that is reality. If he or she doesn't show, move through the situation as smoothly as possible and keep the celebration going.

This is another good argument for giving inexpensive gifts. A five-hundred-dollar gift left unopened is harder to deal with than a five-dollar one. The emotional trauma is difficult enough as it is.

Gifts are the least important part of a holiday or birthday anyway. Family, friends, and good food are the memory makers. If we treat gifts as a minor part of the celebration, we remove one issue that might go wrong.

Protecting Ourselves

Parents are hurt often. They have been disappointed, shocked, insulted, perplexed, and crushed. More than once they have been embarrassed. Understandably they hesitate to put their hand out lest the door is slammed on it again.

It isn't unreasonable for parents to learn to protect themselves. But we also need to take risks. That's what people in relationships do. Even people in shaky relationships may need to do that. Make the effort even if it hurts. But make it a *measured* effort. Know how far you will go and how soon you will back off.

If all you get is an afternoon a year on a holiday, enjoy that afternoon for exactly what it is. Don't try to make up for all the wounded yesterdays. Don't try to recapture the happier days of early childhood, and don't expect the afternoon to launch you into a miraculous tomorrow.

Enjoy the four hours for precisely what they are—a satisfying afternoon with an old friend.

Chapter 12

Forgiving is Difficult

"Does Tyrone have any idea how he has hurt the family?" a mother pondered. "His drinking and lawlessness, his car accidents. I don't think he is even aware of the pain he has caused us. I could forgive him, but I don't know if he has any control over it."

"Sometimes I am tempted to be angry at Lisa," commented a father. "She could have put on her seat belt, and she might still be with us today. Maybe I do hold it against her. I don't know if I have actually forgiven her."

Forgiving is an important value. Most parents would like to reach deep into the well of their heart and forgive their child for anything and everything he or she has done. It sounds simple enough, and it certainly sounds Christian. But brokenhearted parents often have trouble forgiving because the situation is complex.

Yet, if we fail to grapple with the difficulties of forgiving, our healing and future will be in serious jeopardy. Forgiving must not be taken lightly.

It is far easier to forgive the Russians, the Internal Revenue Service, or foreign debt than children. We might forgive robbers, gossips, or arsonists, but children are too close and personal to deal with easily. It is hard to accept that our own child intentionally stabbed us in the back, so to speak.

A child is someone we loved and for whom we sacrificed. Most parents can never imagine hurting a child on purpose, but children seem to hurt themselves, others, and their parents knowingly. It takes a long time for parents to grasp that, if they ever do.

For years we either accepted or made excuses for our child's behavior.

- It's just a phase.
- She didn't mean to do it.
- He has no idea how it hurts us.
- The problem is her group of friends.
- The police are picking on him.
- She is a sensitive child.
- Teenagers are just like that.
- I did some dumb things when I was a kid, too.

When we make such excuses we are deflecting reality. We don't quite know what's going on, but we think our kid is actually a good kid. If an eleven-year-old continually hurts family members, parents are reluctant to hold her responsible. Everyone is sure she will grow out of it and become a fine young lady.

We cannot forgive our child until we can say, "This child has done something wrong and is responsible for her behavior." Consequently, some parents of children who are forty-one years old cannot bring themselves to say, "My child repeatedly, knowingly, and willfully hurts people." That statement is carved over the gateway to forgiveness.

Shirley stood on the front lawn at 11:00 p.m. on graduation night and told her son, "You've got to be back here at 1:00 a.m., and you've got to be sober. If you come in at three or four o'clock

70

drunk, you will hurt your grandparents, your aunt, your dad, and me. Do you understand? One o'clock and sober."

"It's my life," her son replied with anger in his eyes. "It's not my fault if they feel hurt. That's their problem." With that the nineteen-year-old pivoted and walked away.

His mother still feels confused about the confrontation. Was he acting self-centered and cruel toward his relatives? Didn't he have an obligation toward their feelings? Was this simply one more in a long list of wrongs he had callously committed toward the people who loved him?

Shirley can't bring herself to forgive her son because she can't admit that he has done something wrong. And so it goes with millions of parents who waffle over their defiant child's behavior.

More than a hundred years ago Marcel Proust said, "We are healed of a suffering only by experiencing it to the full."[1]

We will not heal until we reach forgiveness. We cannot reach forgiveness until we take a long, full drink of our child's behavior and say, "This is foul, rancid, and disgusting." Then we have put one foot on the road to recovery.

Admitting That We Hate

Lewis B. Smedes' book *Forgive and Forget* (Harper and Row, San Francisco, 1984) is a tough and realistic volume. In his chapter on hate he says, "When we deny our hate we detour around the crisis of forgiveness."

Some of us hate what our child did. We hate what she said. We hate how she treated us. But since she is part of our family, we cannot admit that we hate her and her actions. Consequently, we deny how we feel. If we deny how we feel, forgiving is impossible.

---

1 *The Shorter Bartlett's Familiar Quotations, Permabook Edition* (New York: Little, Brown and Co., 1958), p. 305.

Middle-aged parents stood by the grave of their younger son. As they cried, they felt hatred. They hated what he had done. He was drunk when he drove ninety miles an hour and crashed into a tree. He and his girlfriend were killed, and another friend was critically injured.

These parents can bring themselves to admit that they hate what their son did, but they are afraid to ask whether they hate their son. Instead, their minds dither around as they try to be sympathetic and understanding. "Boys will be boys," they rationalize. "He didn't realize how much he had to drink. Maybe his friends urged him to drive faster. He simply had to sow a few wild oats. Lots of boys do this, but they just happen to miss the tree." Parents are prone to make excuses instead of accepting the facts and admitting their hate.

The message is not that we need to start hating our child. Rather, those of us who *do* hate our child need to accept it, admit it, and move on to forgiveness. The majority of us fit into this group.

We often get angry with people we barely know, like the person who cuts us off on the highway. That anger is usually surface and fleeting. Seldom do we nurse it into deep-seated hate and hold a grudge.

We are more likely to hate those who are near and dear. Hate is frequently reserved for those whom we trust—the people we eat with and sleep with and to whom we tell intimate stories. When they betray our love and commitment, feelings strike to our heart and soul.

We have been hurt by someone we love. It is quite understandable if we hate the person who inflicted that pain.

Choosing to Forgive

If our son has gotten into trouble with the law, stolen from his sisters, moved to Anchorage, and refuses to accept our calls, we are at a loss to know how we feel. Do we love a son who rejects and abuses us? Do we keep reaching out to someone who never reaches back? Do we speak well of him even when we feel the opposite?

Not knowing how to feel about him, we have finally learned to resent him. A decade and a half of outrageous behavior brought us to that point. We have steeled ourselves against our own child. Now we are able to continue life protected from any more of his stones and arrows.

Soon after we have fortified our emotions in this mental cocoon of resentment, someone comes along and asks, "Have you ever forgiven your child?"

Horrors! Does he have any idea what he is asking? First I loved this child from the depths of my heart. Then I forced myself to admit that my child is a creep who cares for no one but himself. Painfully I settled in and accepted those feelings. Now someone says I should consider forgiving my son.

It's like telling someone that even though his emotions have been to sea many times and have sunk every time, he needs to pull up his ropes and go out to sea again.

Parents are called to weigh anchor and sail out on the vessel of forgiveness. Afraid of where forgiveness will lead, parents stay on the shore and clutch on to hate, resentment, or a false sense of innocence and shiver at the thought of giving them up.

For those who choose to use it, forgiveness is available to help. Those who hold on to anger are deprived of freedom by their hate and bitterness. Forgiving is effective only to those who recognize their need for it. No one should try to force us to do something we don't want to do.

Forgiving is a radical approach. It goes against our natural instincts. Vengeance, self-pity, self-protection, callousness, denial, and hate are the normal reactions. Forgiving is a spiritual exercise. Even a nonspiritual person has to enter the realm of spirituality to forgive. It is not the logical inclination of the human mind.

If someone hurts us, we naturally feel the need to hurt back. We want to hurt him to protect ourselves and to teach him a lesson—unless we decide to rise to a spiritual level.

Anyone who has been hurt understands the difficulty in forgiving. Forgiving asks a great deal. Brokenhearted parents understand and are slow to condemn other hurting parents who find it hard to forgive their children.

If a parent forgives an estranged child, does that parent have to open up to be hurt again? Not necessarily. A parent can forgive all of his child's past behavior and still refuse to let that child move back into the house. We can forgive a child and not lend him money again.

Forgiving doesn't mean we surrender our sense of safety. We might forgive an embezzler, but we will not make him president of the bank. We might forgive an alcoholic but we refuse to buy him alcohol. Parents can forgive and still be reasonably cautious, careful, and even watchful.

Benefits of Forgiving

If we can bring ourselves to forgive our child, several benefits will be realized. Each of these could improve our lives.

We won't have to correct yesterday.

Sheila lied to the family and embarrassed everyone at the reunion. For years they waited for her to apologize. Forgiving her would erase the anxious waiting.

We won't have to unravel everything.

A family has never understood how their son could steal five hundred dollars and not return it. Forgiving could allow the family to stop trying to figure out the incident.

We can enjoy today for all it has to offer.

Every day spent with a certain daughter brings back fifteen years of pain and defiance. Forgiving lifts the weight and frees us to make this one day count.

We gain a new sense of freedom.

One of the few ways we have to release ourselves and to release our grown child is to forgive him. We want to distance ourselves from his actions, but we can never do that until and unless we forgive him. Otherwise we are bound together with barbed wire.

We will find emotional and spiritual healing.

Growth will be extremely difficult unless we forgive our son for stealing and wrecking the car five years ago. Our spirit remains tied to the terrible incident that we refuse to let go. We weep over the past because we will not release it.

Spiritual and emotional healing are dependent on our willingness to dismiss the past. We either hold on to the memories or hold on to the person. We cannot hold on to both.

We must acknowledge that forgiving isn't as easy as it sounds. Pious souls who tell us we must forgive have usually failed to walk in the shoes of a brokenhearted parent. Their glib remarks, easy idealism, and prepackaged virtues make it seem as if there is nothing to this forgiving business.

No, we don't have to forgive. We might decide we cannot stand the pain. But if we are unable to find a way to forgive, we will carry a great agony the rest of our lives.

The best way to learn about forgiving is to reach deeply into our own experience. Was there a time when we accepted the forgiveness of our sins in Jesus Christ? Did we welcome the power of God, who cheerfully freed us from our past? Those who have received this gift are able to look inside and wrestle with the difficult questions of forgiveness. God has given us a gift, and now we have the opportunity to give that gift to someone else.

There are parents who cannot forgive because they have never felt forgiven. These parents have a serious spiritual and emotional handicap. But those who have received God's gift have a point of reference, a deep well from which to draw. "Bear with each other and forgive whatever grievances you may have against one another. Forgive as the Lord forgave you." (Col. 3:13).

As brokenhearted parents, we agree not to judge each other. How parents deal with their defiant child is a fragile subject. Those of us who have made mistakes will be slow to tell others what to do. However, since Jesus Christ has forgiven us, it is wise to consider how to forgive our children.

Chapter 13

The Strengths and Weaknesses of Hope

Hope is an easy virtue to tout.

"No matter how dark the night, keep your head high and be optimistic."

"We don't know what the future holds, but we know who holds the future."

A dozen easy and trite slogans come to mind and roll smoothly from our tongues. But sometimes these slogans are the wrong thing to say.

Hope has great potential to heal and lift the spirit. Like medicine, however, hope can be prescribed at the wrong time and under the wrong conditions. If hope is to have meaning, it must be administered with caution. When someone doesn't want to be force-fed hope, we should respect his or her wishes.

"My friends used to hit me over the head with hope like it was a hammer," a businessman from Kentucky recalled. "They tried to make me feel guilty because I didn't think things would turn around and blossom like a rose.

"Every year I would get my hopes up four or five times. 'Oh, my son is about to turn around,' I would say. And I would believe it. I did that for fifteen years. That adds up to sixty or seventy times I forced myself to hope.

"Then somebody tells me that I'm a terrible person if I stop hoping. I know more about hope than most people, and I can tell you it hurts to hope."

The message of hope must never be delivered flippantly. People die. They go to prison. They are never found again. They choose not to call their parents. They kill themselves. They die as alcoholics after fifty years of drinking. They abandon their children and are never heard of again.

A blanket challenge to keep our hopes up is sometimes a dagger to the heart. The words, "Don't worry; eventually Megan will come to her senses," can be cruel if spoken at the wrong time.

Distancing Ourselves from Hope

Do you choose to believe that your son will eventually get a handle on his alcoholism and become close to the family again? For those who decide to hope, the gift of optimism can be tremendous strength. But be a realist. Hope might help, and it might not. Don't think your daughter will turn around merely because you hope it to be so.

The Bible tells a great story about a woman who wanted a child when her husband was old. The prophet Elisha told the woman that the following year she would give birth and hold a son in her arms, and a child was born as the prophet had predicted.

As the child grew older, he soon went out into the field where his father was working. One day the boy cried out, "My head! My head!" He was carried to his mother, and she held him in her lap. Around noon the child died, and she laid him on the bed.

Quickly the mother went to see Elisha who had promised her this son. She said to him, "Did I ask you for a son, my lord? …Didn't I tell you, 'Don't raise my hopes'?" (2 Kings 4:28).

The woman felt that her hopes had been played with. At first she couldn't have a child. Then someone said she would.

Then she lost her child. Hope had proven to be an unhappy roller-coaster ride.

Hope is a sword we dare not brandish about lightly. If hope is raised and one's soul is cut, it will be difficult to hope again. At first hope may be a fresh new friend. But after years of disappointment, it becomes a loser standing on the corner in a frayed suit.

"I always thought I would find the answer," reported an aging father. "I had hope coming out of my ears. 'If only I can get him around one more corner,' I always thought. 'If I can get Jason off drugs. If I can get him into college. If I can take him away for the weekend.' There was always one more 'if.' But none of the 'ifs' worked. Now I'm out of hope. I need to stop hoping for a while."

After years of chasing hope, some old hounds need rest. The next corner or the next attempt probably will not work. Sometimes parents need to sit down, catch their breath, and pursue more realistic dreams.

Suppose you see a man standing on a pier on a foggy night, and you happen to strike up a conversation with him. Before long you ask him what he is doing there.

"Waiting for the mermaids to come ashore," he replies.

"Mermaids?" you gulp.

"Oh yes, I've been coming here for years. I've never met one, but I know mermaids are real. Someday I'll meet one. All I have to do is keep hoping. If a person gives up hope, what does he have left?"

If you were a bright-eyed optimist, a dreamer even, what would you tell this man? Would you encourage him? Would you say that his dreams will come true if he keeps on hoping? Would that be fair?

Perhaps you should say, "It's good to have dreams. But while you are dreaming, it might be smart to keep working, playing with your children, and repairing the gutters at home. It isn't smart to stand here too long hoping mermaids will come."

Letting Hope Be a Surprise

After years of trying to change our child's attitude and situation, the time comes to put hope on a different level. Hope is possible. Although hope isn't *always* possible, it is *often* possible. The time may come when we need to stop pushing hope so hard and let it be a surprise.

If your daughter is going to come home and hug you and say she loves you, let it be a surprise. If your son is going to break his drinking problem, let it be a surprise.

The Bible says, "Hope deferred makes the heart sick, but a longing fulfilled is a tree of life" (Prov. 13:12). If we are sick of hoping because we have always been disappointed, it's time to give it a rest. Let hope sneak up on us at the most unexpected times and really surprise us.

Adjusting Our Hope

The time may have come to take a fresh look at the expectations we once had. Junior isn't going to be president of the student body, and Sally isn't going to sing lead in the school musical. We may not have known that earlier, but we know it now. Junior is divorced, can't hold a job, and does little to support his children. Sally seldom calls or writes, and you suspect she and her boyfriend are using drugs. The time has come to adjust our hopes.

We no longer have hope for a responsible child. Our dream is that our child will be less irresponsible. We no longer hope she will stop living with this guy; our dream is that they will give up drugs. If we can't get together this year, maybe we will at least get news that they are well.

Experiences teach us that hope comes in different sizes and in a variety of colors. Hope is available in giant, large, medium, small, and microscopic. The question may not be whether or not we have hope, but rather what kind of hope we have.

We used to dream of camping with our son. Then we dreamed of merely fishing with him. Eventually we wished we could go for a walk with him in the park. Today our hope is that we could sit down and have one civil conversation. Hope and dreams have a way of adjusting, and we have to adjust with them.

A family near Boulder, Colorado, had normal expectations for their son Brad. At first they hoped he would go to college, find a career, and start a family. They looked forward to playing with their grandchildren.

After Brad's numerous bouts with the law, a serious drinking problem, and several wrecked cars, his parents enrolled him in a vocational school. That was good, they thought. Their son could gain a skill in a solid trade. Soon, however, Brad flunked out of school, began using hard drugs, and moved in with a woman.

Today those same parents are pleased whenever they see Brad clear-eyed. They are encouraged to hear that he pays his bills. The couple's child belongs to the woman, but Brad is not the father. Brad's parents accept the child as their grandchild and shower him with attention whenever they get together.

Parents may have to adapt their dreams if they are going to continue to hope. Life is a trade-off, and some parents need to come to grips with painful compromises.

New Births

There are countless stories of parents who warred with their children for years and eventually found peace. Those are good stories. Each should serve as an encouragement to every parent with a broken heart. Adult children everywhere are turning around and building relationships with their parents.

Peter lives near us. At the age of twenty he capped off a career of hell-raising by serving an eighth-month sentence for auto theft. Today Peter has a dependable job, is married, and is the father of a beautiful little girl. The family is sheltered by two proud, doting grandparents. There was a day when no one who knew this young man would have predicted this peaceful scene, least of all the police.

We hear such stories. New births happen to many parents with broken hearts. Like the first birth, it is often painful and prolonged. But when it is completed, both parents accept the gift with joy and pleasure.

Some of the most dramatic turnarounds have come years after the parents had let go. They released their child not knowing where the future might lead. For those who saw the new birth, they had new reason to praise God.

Ultimately, our hope is in God, not in people. God's character never changes. When we go to sleep tonight, we can be certain that when we open our eyes in the morning, the Lord will be by our side.

Chapter 14

Marriage Damage

Chris graduated from high school in May and left for college in late August. His parents filed for divorce in January. Who would have thought that Cliff and Terri would ever end their twenty-six year marriage? What causes people to do things like that?

Actually, this scenario is all too common. Cliff and Terri gallantly and vigorously fought the teen wars. Their son all but burned the town down, and they devoted most of their energies to rescuing the lad.

Now Chris more or less has his attitude together, but the war doesn't end. The struggle simply shifts into the lives of his parents. Tired, bruised, bewildered, and hurt, Cliff and Terri don't have enough relationship left to carry on.

Across town live Brenda and Todd. Their daughter Marie is serving a year in the penitentiary for theft. They visit Marie once a week. The rest of their spare time is spent raising their two sons at home. Next month Grandmother will come over to watch the boys while Brenda and Todd go to Minneapolis for the weekend. They plan to see a show, do a little shopping, and spend time enjoying each other's company.

What's the difference between the two couples? Why is one relationship rolling along while the other has crashed and burned? The answer is not found in the children. Chris and Marie are very similar. Chris is far from being out of the woods, and Marie has a long way to go to pull herself together. To discover the difference we have to look closely at the couples, not at their children.

Parents with broken hearts can go either way. Marriages under this kind of stress become stronger or weaker, but they never remain the same. There are entirely too many explosions, too many arguments, and too many sleepless nights for relationships to stay unaffected.

Understanding the Relationship

Several factors help determine which way the relationship will bend. Too many couples fail to discuss those factors. More often they just let feelings happen and merely accept whatever fallout those feelings bring. Parents who investigate their emotions and understand them could suffer less marriage damage.

Suffering from Guilt

When one or both parents believe they have caused their child's outrageous behavior, enormous suffering will result. The thought that they have *ruined* their own offspring makes parents sad and despondent. That attitude is likely to make a parent difficult to live with.

If couples are to survive, they must resolve any guilt, true or false, to the best of their ability. Counseling or spiritual help may be necessary to gain firm footing.

The Stress of Blame

- "You were away too much."
- "You didn't talk enough."
- "You never wanted to discipline her."
- "You always said he'd grow out of it."

Few couples travel through the explosive years without taking a verbal swing or two at each other. Since they believe this situation must be someone's fault, they are bound to turn on each other occasionally. Even if they don't make an accusation out loud, they say it to themselves and hold their spouses somehow accountable.

The worst blame is "phantom" blame. A spouse is certain his partner created this turmoil but isn't exactly sure how. Ghosts are the most difficult monsters to corner and capture.

Couples need to discuss blame and resolve it. Marriages will not prosper if spouses hold grudges against each other.

Different Styles of Parenting

Mary usually wanted stricter rules: earlier curfews, closer checks on homework, fewer privileges, more breath checks, limits on use of the car. Her husband, Bill, was more laid-back. He believed in more freedom at an earlier age. His goal was for the teenagers to make their own decisions and accept the responsibility for those choices.

Frequently, parents have diverse views on child raising, and they are often frustrated with each other. Their different styles of parenting come from their experiences, their training, and their personal preferences.

Each parent has plenty of examples of children who grew up with a certain style and who turned into fine men and women.

- "Kevin never had a curfew in his life and look at him."
- "Lisa grew up with lots of supervision and see how she turned out."
- "Ted hardly saw his parents and he's a banker."

And so the arguments go. If parents are unable to find some redeeming quality in their partner's parenting style, underground warfare is highly possible. It is best if each parent can find some strength in what the other parent has to offer.

The "Who Looks Good" Award

The counselor looked sternly at the couple and said, "I have to be frank with you both. Mike, if you had spent more quality time with Gary, it probably wouldn't have gone this far. I know it's too late to hear that, but I'm afraid you have to face up to the facts."

Karen's heart leapt with each word. She was off the hook, she thought. Even the counselor agreed that Mike messed up. Wow, what a sense of relief.

Karen believes she has won the "Who Looks Good" award. A trained professional pointed a finger at her wimpy husband and blamed it on him.

Many of us are busy looking for that kind of confirmation. We want someone to set us free and indict our partner. Unfortunately the "Who Looks Good" award is not a marriage builder. Trying to lift our burden at our spouse's expense does damage.

Explaining Your Decisions

There are plenty of mistakes to go around. Under normal conditions couples create enough friction to test the best of marriages. Under extreme pressure, they are certain to mess up, say things that shouldn't be said, and make poor decisions. All of us have regrets of some kind. If we could do parenting over, we would certainly do it differently.

Parents who are forced to make decisions in the heat of conflict must be willing to discuss the choices they make. They can benefit by talking decisions over as conflicts happen. If not, couples need to talk them over soon afterward. Keep short accounts. Parents who never discuss hard decisions are apt to build up resentments toward each other.

Not that every nit-picking decision should create a crisis. Often, you need to make a pronouncement and let it ride. If every decision is second-guessed to death, few actions will be accomplished.

Keeping the Romance Alive

Bob and Laura said they seldom smiled. All their energies were spent trying to corral their wild daughter or worrying about the situation. They had no spirit or drive left to invest in each other.

Their story is typical. Parents are stunned and bewildered over their child's behavior. All of their strength is directed to solving a huge puzzle that seems only to grow more inscrutable.

Smart couples stop at some point, reassess their own relationship, and decide to preserve their love for each other. They also take a close look at their other children and make a vow to protect their good life and sanity. Making choices like that in the heat of battle will be a great help in saving the marriage.

Auto mechanics say we do not change the oil in our cars to protect them for the first 50,000 miles but for the second 50,000. By the same token, parents cannot afford to say, "We will neglect our marriage for the next six years and devote ourselves to Junior. Then when he has left for the Army we will renew our romance." By ignoring the needs of the present, we may be wrecking the hope of the future.

This sounds exhausting, and it is. How can we be all things to all people? Maybe we can't. But neither can we afford to stop our family and pour all our resources into one individual or into one problem. Relationships often do not survive that kind of overload.

Being Kind and Understanding

Mother is too patient; father is too harsh. Mother said something terrible; father promised too much. Mother wants to give him more time; father wants to throw him out. Mother wants to seek professional help; father wants him to go to boarding school.

Those are typical scenarios. Every parent can remember when the other said or did something with which they totally greed. Nevertheless, loving couples try to remain kind and understanding. They still go out to dinner together. They continue to go to church where people love them. They sign up together for tennis lessons. They know their love cannot be shelved for the next five or ten years.

Parents under pressure can read 1 Corinthians 13 and be reminded that

- love is patient;
- love is kind;
- love is not easily angered;
- love keeps no record of wrongs;
- love always protects;
- love always trusts;
- love always hopes;
- love always perseveres.

These are the virtues that jump out to parents with broken hearts. They are reassurances that love can be sorely tested yet prosper.

Righting the Ship

Imagine yourself on a ship riding a tumultuous sea. The continuous rocking soon causes the cargo to shift to one side of the vessel. Quickly the entire crew rushes to grab the loose cargo. As everyone hustles to one side of the ship, it suddenly lists dangerously to that side.

The vessel is now in a perilous position. If everything and everyone remains crammed in one corner of the ship, there is a definite possibility the vessel will capsize. Everyone could be dumped into the ocean if balance is not regained. The crew must quickly move back toward the center and take along whatever it can.

Likewise, if every member of the family rushes over to rescue the erring youth and the family *remains* there, the damage could be considerable.

Chapter 15

Sibling Problems

"I suppose I looked the situation over and made my own choice," a young man from Georgia recounted. "My older brother was tearing up the community and making life miserable for my parents. I decided there was more to gain by getting closer to my poor parents.

"Before long I found it easier to tell on my brother. My parents acted like I was special because I kept pretty clean and spied on Evan. Sometimes my brother caught me, but in the long run I got more out of making it look like I was on my parents' side.

"Actually, I wasn't all that upset at my brother. He didn't treat me that badly. I just tried to figure what I had to do so I could survive."

Every sibling is affected by a brother or sister's behavior. That's fairly obvious. What we can't say for certain is exactly how that effect will manifest itself. And we can't know without listening to each individual sibling.

"I hated it," a young woman remembered. "It seemed like each teacher would greet me in class by saying, 'Well, I hope you aren't like your sister.' After a few years like that, I finally gave up and became like my sister."

It is probably true that our siblings have as much influence on our lives as our parents. They go a long way toward molding our values and life choices. Not that they predetermine how we act, but they certainly are part of the serious tug-of-war.

Resenting the Offender

Frequently a sibling dislikes his brother or sister's disruptive behavior because of the pain it brings. The defiant youth usually hurts himself, his parents, and his siblings. Brothers and sisters become distraught and wish they could prevent all three from being hurt. But, realistically, they may not be able to stop any of the hurt and they become frustrated and angry as a result.

"What I resented most," said Emily "was how it hurt my parents and the burden it placed on me. I couldn't afford to get in trouble at school or wreck the car because my parents couldn't take any more pain.

"My brother burned the town down, and I had to be a little Goody Two-shoes. His actions were so extreme that there wasn't any room left for me to act up.

"I had no desire to compete with my brother even if I could," Emily continued. "I could only try to be as outstandingly good as he was outstandingly awful.

"I went out for sports, was on the honor roll, and joined the choir. For me that was the answer to the question, 'You aren't going to be like your brother, are you?' My life would show them that I wasn't like him.

"In some ways it even made me a better person. I think I tried harder because he didn't try at all. Maybe I owe him a little bit for that, but not much."

Generally, life would have gone much more smoothly if this brother and sister had been civil. Holidays are frequently tense and unpredictable. Sometimes rules are stricter because of someone's outrageous behavior. Siblings often feel embarrassed at school, at church, or in the neighborhood. Even finances can be more limited because of a wrecked car, extra hospital bills, fines, or unnecessary setbacks. Siblings see their parents angry or in tears. A cloud frequently hangs over the family when a brother or sister is a constant problem.

The last thing in the world teens want is a weird family member. They don't want parents who dress funny. They don't want a pink flamingo statue in the front yard. And they certainly don't want a brother or sister who walks on the wild side.

Young people think the pimples on their noses are the size of volcanoes, and they believe everyone is staring straight at them. The last thing they want is a sibling who stands out.

It's easy for an adult to say, "Don't worry, everyone knows you aren't like that." That's only a small part of the issue. The teen years are for blending. A rebellious sibling makes it almost impossible to hide in a crowd.

Trying to Intercede

Sibling love mixed with idealism will lead many brothers and sisters to try to pull a rebellious youth out of the mud. A few are successful, but the vast majority only get hurt more seriously for their efforts.

"I did try," Ted told us. "I lectured my brother. I tried to get him up in the mornings. I threw out the alcohol hidden in his dresser. None of it worked. Finally I just became more angry at him. If I would admit it, I'm pretty bitter today over what he did."

Frequently siblings will attempt to act indifferent. They hate to acknowledge three things: they care about their sibling; they feel hurt themselves, and they hate to see their parents hurt. If they do something to intercede, they are letting one or more of those feelings take charge. Since they are uncomfortable with those feelings, they resent the fact that they have responded to them, leading to even greater resentment of their brother or sister.

Ultimately, trying to fix the rebellious youth often results in a strong sense of failure and guilt. The sibling knows the upheaval wasn't his fault, but like other family members, he wonders what he should have done to turn it around. For decades a sibling may wrestle silently with two uncomfortable positions. On the one hand, he knows he could not have changed the situation. On the other hand, he feels responsible for not having changed it.

The sooner siblings are told the truth, the better. Someone they respect needs to look them in the eye and tell them it wasn't their fault. They suspect that might be the case, but they still need a firm voice to say it out loud.

Blaming Parents

Children, even teenagers, like to see their parents as big, strong, wise figures. They want to believe parents can solve life's larger problems, especially when those problems center in the home. When this does not happen, blaming the parents is normal.

"My sister quit school when she was sixteen. She was a strong-headed troublemaker. I realize she was going nowhere. But deep inside I probably still blame my parents for letting her quit. I know they couldn't keep her in school, and I know they tried. But somehow I see them as weak and failing all of us by not holding her there."

Possibly this is one of the chinks in our parents' armor that none of us wants to see. And yet all of us see it one way or another. If our parents had been perfect, we think, they could have stopped this. We know our parents aren't perfect, and yet somehow that seems beside the point.

When we hit our late twenties or early thirties, we learn to accept the truth. Our parents may have tried desperately to change the situation. The fact that it did not improve may have very little to do with our parents' efforts or abilities. The best of intentions are seldom enough to slow a runaway train. It may simply have to run out of fuel.

Most families will never be able to pinpoint a single reason why a teenager went wild. Lots of young people drink alcohol, have trouble learning, have fathers who are away at work, and yet they don't go off the charts with a defiant lifestyle. To say that a family member became rebellious because he started hanging around with a kid named Tyler is too simplistic. Many young people with similar circumstances remain within the boundaries of acceptable behavior.

As long as the precise reason for the extreme behavior remains a mystery, the family will be uneasy. From time to time we will cast suspicious eyes at each other.

Did his sister spoil him? Did his brother pick on him too much? Was Dad too firm? Was Mom too lenient? Was the school too lax? Were the police too strict? Or was it simply the teen's series of terrible judgment calls?

Occasionally blame raises its ugly head and travels around the family. That uneasy feeling may never go away entirely.

The best hope for siblings is to accept yesterday as unchangeable. We will not be able to dig up yesterday and fix it. The more important question is, "What now?" How do we interact and build relationships today?

Moving On

The apostle Paul sets a high standard when he says, "Forgetting what is behind and straining toward what is ahead…" (Phil. 3:13).

This doesn't mean families should forget problems and not talk about them. Siblings need to air their feelings. Some questions can be dealt with and resolved. Discussions may clear things up without actually finding answers.

At least family members might be able to explain their actions or inaction. Even if the sibling strongly disagrees with that action, at least he or she can hear it out. Even though the total mystery may never be solved, a few clouds might be chased away. Possibly a sibling needs to shout at his father, "Why did you keep giving him the keys?" Merely expressing what is bottled up in the heart can be of enormous benefit.

Siblings often suffer from a Cain/Abel syndrome. Cain rebelled, acted out, became outrageous. In his defiant attitude toward God, he made his innocent brother Abel pay the ultimate price of death. That was unfair. All in the family suffer when a family member goes too far.

Every suffering sibling should have the opportunity to express his frustration at the unfairness of the situation. That won't change history, but it will allow the person to have a voice.

Chapter 16

Where Was God?

The most important question raised by anyone who suffers loss may be "Where was God?" If we lose our job, watch a child die, get divorced, or have our heart broken in any way, this question bobs to the top: *Why did God allow this terrible thing to happen?* Some people lose their faith over this mystery. Others are stunned by it. Fortunately, many give it serious thought and discover an even richer faith.

The question deserves careful consideration. Naturally, we look inside to see if we are rotten enough to deserve this sad outcome. Did God pour down His wrath on our family because we didn't go to church enough, didn't give enough, or committed some spiritual transgression?

The answer is God rarely acts that way. Basically, God is in the grace, love, forgiveness, and redemption business. If our heavenly parent were out to get us, He could bring continuous, unbearable pain. But His nature is to be generous rather than mean-spirited. If revenge were God's practice, He would bring loss to cheats, swindlers, and other malefactors. The fact is many evil people prosper and many good people hurt.

Do you picture God as a cruel dictator, eager to condemn His children and wrack them with pain? If so, you need to take a new look at the loving Father who sent his Son to die for us. The goodness of God is His strong virtue. He loves each person in moments of grief *and* in moments of happiness.

Praying for Change

Brokenhearted parents learn to pray. It's one of those peculiar gains that comes their way. If we haven't prayed for years, the urgent desire to pray returns the first night our teenager fails to come home. And when we pray, we gather every fiber of hope and faith that we can muster.

Sometimes young people get a grip and turn around, but many times they do not. Some remain renegades for years, and others distance themselves forever.

Eventually, we ask ourselves or we ask God why He didn't move in and change the situation. As parents we did what was spiritually right. We prayed. We felt more spiritual. We may have attended church a bit more. We might have given a few extra dollars to the Lord's work. Apparently the result of these spiritual exercises was zip. Nothing. Our teen plunged deeper and deeper into a poor lifestyle.

The problem is that we asked God to change another person. God is big on changing people who want to be changed, but He also seems willing to let most people make their own moral choices. God rarely elects to take away the power of choice.

When we pray that the Lord will change someone else, we are almost always praying for the wrong goal. If that worked, we could pray all day for the crooks, murderers, and deviants of this world and see them change their ways. We are usually unable to alter our child's behavior by prayer. Prayer has the potential to move mountains, but little prospect for changing other people.

It's a shame that we may see our faith in God wane for a while because of His apparent silence. That's a terrible blow to our spiritual walk, but our faith will most likely return. Our faith was bruised because we believed and hoped we could change others through prayer. That premise is misinformed.

Never again will I pray that God will change someone else. More realistically, we must pray that God will change *us*. By praying that prayer, we are laying ourselves open before God and asking for new direction. We are asking for help to become more patient, understanding, loving, firm, steadfast, and forgiving. The Lord is eager to accommodate this kind of request.

God does answer prayer. Prayer does change things. But most of all, it changes the person who prays. If we understand that, our faith in Christ, our closeness to the Holy Spirit, and our confidence in prayer will remain intact.

Parents with broken hearts will change. They can't go through this much trauma and remain the same. The real question is *how* they will change. The Lord can enable them to determine which way they will we go.

If we turn to the Lord, we can avoid bitterness, despair, and hopelessness. God can help us achieve acceptance, love, and peace. Those are real attitudes worth seeking and achieving. They are part of the fruit of the Spirit and are attainable even in the most painful circumstances.

The Community of Suffering

The Lord has many children who are seriously delinquent and rebellious. He calls them to himself as a hen gathers her chicks, but they will not come. Because of that, God's heart is broken.

Parents who suffer a similar loss understand something of what our heavenly Father has endured. To that extent we identify better with that sad corner of God's heart, and He with ours. We can be drawn closer to God by experiencing pain.

henomenon is called the community of suffering. No one understands a parent who has lost a child in death like another parent who has endured the same trial.

God has many prodigal sons and daughters. The loss of each, even if temporary, causes terrible pain. Naturally the Lord understands us, but through this agony, we may also understand Him better.

Encouraging One Another

Parents with broken hearts often discover what is most important in life. They know that real values are not material. Materialism fails in times of family loss. At these times, many of us are likely to seek spiritual values, which we now perceive as the most worthwhile.

As a result, parents often become more sensitive to the pain experienced by other families and individuals. They are more eager to reach out and help a faltering friend. They are more likely to hold the hand of someone whose child has been arrested, quit school, or run away. It's harder to stand by and say nothing when you have a fair understanding of what they are going through.

Others find spiritual service in teaching a parenting class, leading a youth group, or rounding up a group of kids and doing things together. These are all spiritual services because they do the work of God as His Spirit moves His people to care for others.

One of the worst ways for parents to react is to fold up and feel useless because their child is in rebellion. Though they may feel like failures, that's no reason to run from God and His service. Parents may be wounded, but that is not sufficient cause to drop out of a meaningful life.

A Christian speaker and conference leader in the Midwest simply lets the truth hang out. He doesn't tell the gory details, but he lets the conferees know that his family has its share of problems. He even adds that there has been trouble with the police. Because he is up front without pouting, many people feel that his ministry is all the more effective. They welcome leadership from someone who has traveled those same rapids.

Today we are more likely to encourage wounded Christians to continue in spiritual service. We are less judgmental and more accepting. God loves the brokenhearted, and many fellow Christians do too.

In the movie *Shadowlands,* C. S. Lewis is depicted as an authority on pain. He had written and lectured extensively on how God relates to suffering. However, Lewis's friends were skeptical, since he had dealt with little personal pain except for his mother's death. He knew a great deal about the subject, but almost nothing about the experience.

Eventually, Lewis married, and his wife became very ill. From that moment on, the author was intimately acquainted with love, loss, and pain. Too soon she died of cancer. The school of life taught Lewis a lesson no textbook could offer.

Parents with broken hearts are learning about God in a way they could not have otherwise known. Instead of God and parents rejecting each other, they often embrace one another as fellow travelers on the journey of pain.

Chapter 17

What We've Gained

The gain is not worth the pain. Parents aren't glad their child went to prison in spite of their having learned valuable lessons through the experience. Whatever virtue, whatever strength, whatever insight they may have gained they would gladly give back if they could reshape the past ten or fifteen years.

It's much like struggling to keep your business afloat and finally going bankrupt. When everything is sold and closed, your accountant reminds you that there are some tax benefits coming your way. Naturally you accept the benefits, but you would much rather have had a successful business.

One of the characteristics of the Christian life is finding good in life's experiences. Many parents with broken hearts can count their blessings despite their grief. Let's take a look at some of those blessings.

We learn humility.

During the early months and years we fight for our pride and we defend the children we love. No one faults a parent for trying to preserve the family. But eventually we learn how little we can control. Our teenager flunks school, is arrested, goes to jail, gets pregnant, or fails in some other way. Reality demonstrates there is so much we can't control.

Humility begins to set in. We realize how limited we are. In spite of our education, our experience, our finances, our spirituality, our connections, and our best intentions, there is almost nothing we can do.

It's a devastating feeling, and it doesn't come quickly. It's often after the second arrest, the second wrecked car, the second rehab session, and writing the fifteenth check that we finally understand we can't change the situation.

Our own sense of inadequacy settles in. We are humbled by our inability to alter another person's life. Our limits scream out to us. We sit on an ash heap and accept ourselves for who we are. "For I eat ashes as my food and mingle my drink with tears" (Ps. 102:9).

We lose our idealism.

Parenting is an optimistic venture. Whether by birth or by adoption, we welcome children because we have hope. We believe in cowboy shirts and patent leather shoes. We believe in piggyback rides and high school graduations.

We know that not all dreams come true. We know that life can have a nasty bite to it, but our idealism makes us appreciate life's gifts and blessings. They don't come equally, and they don't come automatically.

We become less judgmental.

We used to know the answers. We knew what other parents should do. For the life of us, we couldn't understand why they didn't just *do* something. Some of us were glib with solutions like:

- "Just take the keys away."
- "They wouldn't do that in my house."
- "That kid needs to be taught some respect."
- "I'd put him in the homework business."
- "She wouldn't sneak out of my house twice."

Now we know better. When we hear of a family that's having teen trouble, we feel for them. Sometimes we try to encourage them; sometimes we pray for them; sometimes we ask if we can help, but seldom do we judge them.

We strengthen our marriage.

Chris and Brenda from the Midwest said the worst year of their marriage and the best year of their marriage was the same year. Chris said, "I would tell Brenda, 'Look, Rachel won't come home until at least midnight. There isn't anything we can do until then. Why don't we go out to eat and see a movie? Sitting around, worrying about her all evening will only hurt us more.'"

It doesn't work that way for everyone. Many marriages disintegrate under the pressure. Fortunately, some couples realize how much their love for each other means to them.

Disruptive children can create an unstable atmosphere at home. Sometimes rifts occur between siblings as well as between siblings and parents. Often parents do not survive these emotional agonies. Couples who do weather those lengthy storms are thankful for the stronger love they now possess. Because experience can work like strands in a rope, hardship and disappointment frequently make love's cord stronger.

We stop blaming each other.

"Because we were his parents, we thought the blame had to be in us," Todd explained. "First, we looked inside ourselves for the answers. Then we decided it was the other parent's fault."

Our society has long taught that children are the product of their parents. We have learned that good traits, as well as bad ones, come directly from them. If we believe that, we will eventually cast an accusing eye at each other.

"It got so bad," Linda volunteered, "that I was pleased when someone said anything that put my husband down. If someone said, 'You know, Ben doesn't talk much,' in my mind I'd say, *'That's it. If he had talked more, this wouldn't have happened.'* Or I'd blame it on his being so frugal. I had to find flaws in poor Ben so I wouldn't take all the blame myself."

Under the most pleasant conditions it's easy to exaggerate the shortcomings of our spouse. With family stress, we are even more likely to devalue our partner and actually accuse him or her. Couples who survive learn to stop blaming each other. They know their relationship is too important to destroy.

We learn how our heavenly Father feels.

Parents experience a taste of the excitement God has for His children. But parents with broken hearts also get a glimpse of how their heavenly Father must feel when rebellious and estranged children frustrate Him.

Having estranged children leaves a gut feeling that no class, seminar, or study can duplicate. There is no other way to know but to experience it. This estrangement didn't happen to us so we could *have* that feeling. But since we have experienced it, we can now identify with a side of God's nature that otherwise we would not know.

Reading the story of the prodigal son cannot compare with living that story. God lives it daily. We have now lived at least part of it.

Jesus said, "How often I have longed to gather your children together, as a hen gathers her chicks under her wings, but you were not willing" (Matt. 23:37). We understand that text now—not in our heads, but in our hearts. Many times we would have gathered our child into our loving arms, but the young person was not willing.

We now have some idea how it makes our heavenly Father feel when we wander away. We also understand more about the joy God feels when we move closer to Him.

We are more tolerant.

Our bruises have made us more understanding of the mistakes of other parents. We are not necessarily more tolerant of young people, but we are more tolerant of their parents.

Many parents with bad experiences think parents should be stricter with all youth. We know it's hard to be consistent. We know it's tough to make four or five crucial decisions every evening. We know it's difficult to stay ahead of a plotting, deceptive, bright young person who believes all adults are to be fooled.

When a father or mother sits at home, head in hands, crying, we are unlikely to chew that parent out for his or her behavior.

We learn lessons in courage.

Soldiers, missionaries, and policemen are supposed to excel in courageous acts. Parents are expected to show courage when doctors in hospital rooms say they have to operate on their children. But little did they know they would need courage just to answer the phone, to confront their own children, and just to face the next day.

A father in Tulsa said, "I was standing on a golf course around the fifth hole when I happened to look toward the clubhouse and see a police car pull into the lot. Instinctively I thought, 'Oh no, what now?' 'Why else would there be a police car except that my son is in trouble again, and they have come for me?' The policeman wasn't looking for me at all. I remained shaken for the rest of the round even after the police car drove away.

"Every day I needed to dig up the courage to go on with a normal life. Some days I didn't want to deal with the uncertainties and the fears, but I had to find a way."

Courage is only a topic of conversation until we are forced to call on its power. Highly rebellious young people make us grapple with virtues we otherwise might ignore.

We wrestle with forgiveness.

The brokenhearted are forced to make sense out of forgiveness, even though they probably never master it. Whom do they forgive? When do they forgive? How do they forgive someone who has not changed his ways? Do they forgive someone who doesn't even want to be forgiven? Does God forgive us based on our ability or willingness to forgive our own children?

Everyone supports the idea of forgiving. The basis of our Christian faith is that we are forgiven. But when we feel hurt, betrayed, abused, and mistreated, it is hard to forgive, especially when foolish actions continue.

Corrie ten Boom taught a valuable lesson about forgiving. She said she learned to forgive the prison guards while she was still in the concentration camp. She didn't wait until she was free and then forgive them upon reflection. The grace of God allowed her to forgive them in the middle of their acts of cruelty.

Christ forgave His tormentors while He was being crucified. His example calls us to an incredibly high standard. However successful or unsuccessful we may be, we have been given an opportunity to have one of life's richest experiences. We have felt pain while we held forgiveness in our hands and tried to decide what to do with it. Without this agony, we may never have had to make that vital decision.

To this extent, rebellious, even defiant children have brought true wealth to our souls. Not that we wanted it. Not that we have made the best use of these virtues. But we can be grateful for the side benefits.

Automobile accidents make us more cautious. Lost investments make us wiser. Pulled muscles make us careful. In the same way, belligerent children can make us stronger. Each parent has to decide how much he or she will draw on these newfound character qualities.

"If the truth were known," wrote a man from Omaha, "I owe my son a great deal. For all the pain he brought into our lives, his actions opened the doors so blessings could fly in at the same time. I will probably never be able to explain it to him correctly. I probably will never try. But in a backhanded sort of way, he has blessed my life. He made me a better person.

"He changed the way I see others. My values aren't the same. I wish I could have learned the same lessons while he was a good kid, but that route was closed to me. Nevertheless I am, begrudgingly, grateful for the good that his bad behavior brought my way."

Chapter 18

If They Had Advice to Give

Advice isn't easy to give or to accept. Many parents in stress struggle to find their own path through their ordeal. Only after the storm has passed do they wish good advice had been available.

But there are exceptions. Some parents are looking for help from other parents, and they are willing to try it. For their sake, I have asked brokenhearted parents what advice they might give.

Brokenhearted parents have learned a great deal. Out of their experiences came a dozen suggestions for parents who are in the early stages of the battle. The advice below is in no particular order of importance.

Let your child fail early.

This is hard advice for parents of a 14-year-old rebellious child. Parents try so hard to keep their children from pain. But that's a serious mistake. If a teenager breaks something, that same teen must fix it.

"I fought hard to make sure he graduated from high school. He drank, didn't go to class, flunked exams, and generally ignored the system. Looking back, I know it was a loss of reality to prop him up and keep him from the consequences of his misbehavior," a parent told us.

This is a difficult decision. Some teens snap out of their rebellion. Others merely bounce from problem to problem. At some point a parent has to decide when to remove the safety nets.

Use tough love.

In danger of becoming a worn-out phrase, tough love is nevertheless essential. One father said, "Take the car keys away whether they hate you or not. Many times we should have."

It's hard to be tough with someone you love. Most of us think if we give love, we will receive love in return. When we give love to our child and get contempt in return, the transaction confuses us.

Tough love forces itself to draw a line and makes itself keep that line.

"The first time he stayed out all night," a mother told us, "I disciplined him a little. He thought that was no big deal, so a few weeks later he did it again. Then I said, 'No more nice guy,' and laid down the law. Until then I thought that if I treated him nice, he'd treat me nice."

Reduce expectations.

Every family expects to be a neat little unit. None of us planned to be the Ma Barker family with children running around robbing banks. We need to accept the facts. Half of our children may divorce. One of our children may be arrested or get pregnant. Our children are likely to try drugs. They might marry someone who will avoid your family. A loving 20-year-old might suddenly change dispositions and blame her parents for ruining her life. A son might move across the country and not contact you for five years.

We shouldn't think our family is too good, too loving, too Christian, too educated, too middle-class, or too anything for this to occur. The average, normal family has problems. The kid we think is an excellent student and a responsible person at age 11 could later turn any way he or she chooses to go. Remember, life can take a sudden jolt.

Live one day at a time.

Is the sun shining? Can you do something you would enjoy with your spouse or a child? Do it today. There is no telling what you might have to deal with tonight or tomorrow. Don't live in fear, but be careful to use the goodness you can find in this present hour.

The Book of Proverbs teaches, "Do not boast about tomorrow, for you do not know what a day may bring forth" (27:1). Every distressed parent knows the truth of this passage. Each day can be filled with its own surprises and disappointments. Don't live desperately, grasping at every hour. Instead live gladly, knowing how important the present moment is.

Communicate clearly.

Say what you mean and mean what you say. Many parents are literally afraid to talk.

- We don't know what to say.
- We are afraid we will say too much.
- We are afraid we will say too little.
- We are afraid we will cry or shout.

We are held as verbal hostages. Our child's misbehavior so intimidates us that we are afraid anything we say will be held against us. Parents are often reluctant to say what they feel because they don't want to say the wrong thing. A parent might be angry, confused, disappointed, fed up, frustrated. She may believe she is being treated like trash. But she doesn't want to say any of that. Too often we swallow our words and fail to share our feelings.

Every child needs to know how his or her parents feel. Children have a right to hear the pleasant feelings. They also have an absolute, unquestionable need to hear the bad news. Start off in small chunks, if necessary. Move from words to sentences to paragraphs. Everyone in the family needs to hear how Mom and Dad are honestly affected by his or her behavior.

A typical reaction of parents after their children have moved out is: "I wish I had communicated better and more often."

Say, "I love you."

Take your hostile, defiant teenager by the shoulders, look him in the eye, and say, "I love you and I always will." He may shrug it off and back away, but he needs to hear it. Even if he reacts negatively, he has to have those words stored in his memory bank.

A young man came home after drinking heavily and staying out all night. His dad put his arms around the boy and said, "Son, I love you, and I am willing to do whatever it takes to deal with your problems. We're in this together."

The boy shrugged his shoulders and went to his room. The next night he came to his dad and said, "I'm ready for help now."

Do it and do it often. If a daughter is cold and distant, she can't afford to have a parent who becomes cold and distant, too. Say it when it hurts to say it. Do it through tears if necessary, but do it! That's what parents with broken hearts say.

"Sometimes it was terribly hard to say," recounted a father from Kansas City. "But I said it. Other times I left a note on his dresser or on the steps to his room. If we were going to argue over everything else, I didn't want there to be any doubt about this."

Often we feel foolish telling someone we love her when she has nothing civil to say to us. She may lie to us, steal from us, embarrass us, cause us pain. And yet we still have to let her know we love her. It's not that we say it every time. But we must say it enough to make it register.

"I say it every time I write him," a mother declared. "I haven't seen him for a couple of years, but I still write. And I end each letter with, 'Remember, I will always love you,' and I mean it."

Show affection.

Porcupine teenagers may not like to be hugged. They may be terribly difficult to put our arms around, but many parents wish they had done it more often. Typically, parents become huggers, holders, and even kissers after they have had trouble with one child. Then they determine to embrace the other children still at home. Clearly, they wish they had the rebellious child around to hug. Seeing their lack of demonstrated affection as a mistake, they have promised themselves not to make it again.

An older boy complained to his parents, "You love my sisters more than you love me, don't you?" His sisters were younger and still in what the parents felt was the cuddly stage. Their son noticed the difference and evidently thought he wasn't too old for a cuddle now and then too.

"My son was standing alone by the kitchen door, his face taut, his shoulders rigid. I could tell his mind was pulling apart, trying to decide whether to obey or to grab the doorknob and run away for another evening. I walked over, lump in my throat, and put one arm around that bubbling volcano. It was the only thing I could do."

Another dad said, "Whenever we get together, my son will give me a hug. He won't say much, but he will give me a hug."

"I'd try to hug him in the morning before he left," a mother added. "He always seemed so down, and a hug was all I could do."

Love unconditionally.

That's the goal. Sometimes it's just the ideal.

A man who was an alcoholic for thirty years before becoming a Christian is disappointed that his parents didn't accept him unconditionally, even when he was drinking so heavily. In all fairness to his parents, consider what he did. He continually came home at all hours falling-down drunk. The man stank from booze and urine. Repeatedly he threw up all over the house and wet the bed, couch, and carpets. His behavior hurt his parents' health and drove his brothers and sisters away.

The man wrecked cars, seriously injured a passenger, was repeatedly arrested, rushed into a marriage and then divorced. Frequently he left home and didn't contact his parents for years. Decades later, he holds it against his parents for not accepting him unconditionally. That would have been nice, but it's asking a great deal. The question should not be, can we *accept* children but rather, can we *love* them?

This is a tall order to fill. Many parents continue to love unconditionally under the most horrendous of circumstances. That is the best way if they can pull it off. No doubt it is the kind of love God has for His children. No doubt we would all be better off if we had it. And yet every parent is sympathetic to those who find such love difficult to maintain.

As difficult as it may be for parents to give unconditional love, let us recommend they *try* it. God loves us even in our rebellion. God's love is consistent even when we turn our backs on Him. We need to get as close to that kind of love as we can. On that basis we can begin to deal with unconditional love for our children. Parents with broken hearts are humble enough to know how tough that is.

Let your child express anger.

Temper outbursts and extreme anger are shocking at first. In some children, the hostility begins with the onset of the teen years. Others seem angry even as preschoolers. There is no magic time when young people begin to go into rages.

When parents first see it, they are usually confused. How could their innocent child express all this vile anger? We think it is temporary and will soon pass away. Sometimes we ignore it. At other times we come down hard and demand that they cool it.

Unfortunately, for some families the madness doesn't go away. It might even increase in intensity and frequency. When this happens, parents often become frightened, but veteran parents tell us not to be intimidated by the anger. Let them be mad. Parents have to draw lines and set boundaries. Even if their youth resents it and throws fits, the parents must not remove boundaries.

Young people need to get angry, and adults need to let them. The anger could get out of hand, and the adult may need help from the authorities. But a parent must remain firm and let the youth vent his hostility as long as it is not physically harmful. Venting is a hopeful sign that could lead to understanding and resolution.

Parents may have to decide whether to lock their bedroom door to protect themselves against their own angry child. Many parents are driven to this point. But if we retreat every time a child becomes angry, he will learn how to frighten and control his own parents. Parents have to stand up and let their young persons be angry.

Never hit your adolescent child.

Adults who hit adolescents are courting disaster. They have challenged that young person either to hit back or run. Almost never do parents win a physical confrontation. Even if they win the fight, they will almost certainly lose the teenager. The temptation to hit can become overwhelming, but don't yield. Protect yourself if necessary, but do not hit an adolescent.

Tell it like it is.

"When Todd was arrested, I went to my Bible study group the next night and told them exactly what had happened. I couldn't cope with the problem and try to cover it up at the same time. I simply didn't have the energy," a father told me.

Often other people know more about the situation than their parents, and more people know than we might think. It's best to assume that everyone knows about your child's problem and act accordingly. That doesn't mean we owe everyone an explanation or a detailed account. However, it is usually futile to try to keep it a big secret. Remember:

- You can't keep it a secret.
- Some people need to know so they can help.
- You have more important, more immediate things to tend to.

"All I could think of was, *What if Grandmother finds out?* If I had it to do all over again, I'd tell Grandmother the first day," said a lady from the Midwest.

Learn to laugh and enjoy life.

It's the last thing you feel like doing, but it has to be done. If a parent shuts down and stops living, the situation will degenerate more rapidly. Not only will the parents be hurt, but so will the siblings.

A young person's defiant lifestyle could last a year or two. On the other hand, his behavior might remain outrageous for a decade or two. For some it might never turn around. In the face of that potential, are we willing to give up our happiness because our child is in a rebellious stage? There are parents who elect never to smile again. They have allowed a bad situation to poison everything around them.

"I felt like a combat chaplain," one father observed. "While everything was blowing up around me, I had to remain calm, cheerful, and optimistic. It's the only way to go."

Some situations we cannot change. We cannot make the bad times into good times, but God has given us the ability to find joy amidst our pain.

Many parents wish they had had a dozen hints when their troubles started. Instead, they had to learn everything the hard way. Their hope is that others will benefit from their experience. Above these dozen bits of advice there is one overruling guideline to keep in mind. Both parents and rebellious young people agree on this bit of wisdom: *Don't blame yourself.*

Many young people come back to tell their parents there wasn't anything they could have done. The child chose the defiant life, and he was determined that no one would stop him.

We hurt everyone involved by blaming ourselves. Assigning blame usually only makes the constructive process more difficult.

The main question to answer is: Where do we go from here?

Chapter 19

Looking for Purpose

I asked a woman whose son had been involved in years of rebellious and destructive behavior if I could interview her for this book.

"This may be exactly what I've been looking for," she replied as she began to cry. "I've prayed for years that there might be some purpose to all of this. Maybe God will help others through the book."

The search for purpose is typical among parents with broken hearts. Most were taught that God has a purpose for everything in life. Believing that the Lord could have intervened at any time, they feel He must have had a reason for not turning around their son or daughter.

"One of my twin daughters died two years ago," a gray-haired gentleman reported. "Don't think I haven't looked almost every day for God's reason for taking her life."

It is a healthy sign when a parent tries to find something good in loss and tragedy. The very question of purpose suggests that the parent wants to make sense out of life. He or she wants to find some way to turn a loss into a gain. The gain may be for others rather than for himself, and although the gain will never erase or justify the loss, the hope is that the disaster will not be a total waste.

Brokenhearted parents also want to reaffirm their belief in God. A terrible disappointment has crashed into their lives, and they want to maintain their faith despite this horror. By asking God for direction and purpose, they continue in their decision to walk close to Him.

Purpose, meaning, faith, faithfulness, trust, and service are concepts that flood the believer's heart and mind. Parents want to find comfort in their continued dedication to these concepts.

Letting Go of "Why?"

Too often we are bogged down trying to discover the answer to "Why?" The question is normal, but it may get in the way of our ability to accept the facts and find purpose in the future.

- Why did God take her?
- Why did our son reject our love?
- Why did she have to marry him?
- Why didn't God stop my son?

Usually, we seek answers to the why question in three directions.

- Why did our child do what he did?
- Why didn't we do enough to prevent this?
- Why didn't God intervene?

It is as if a ranch hand kept a horse in a corral only to wake up one morning and discover the mare gone. The gate to the corral stands wide open. If the wrangler sits on the trough and asks why the gate was open, he probably is wasting his time. *Did he leave the gate ajar? Did the horse learn to work the lever? Did God open the gate?* How long will the wrangler sit around asking those questions?

The answer to the questions may never be found. And if by some miracle the reason is discovered, what will change? If the wrangler solves the mystery, will the horse return gladly to the corral? Obviously the answer is no. No amount of soul searching will correct the past. Now that the horse has bolted, the only appropriate question is: "What now?"

Sometimes we question in an attempt to redo the past. Sometimes we do it to avoid facing the present. And sometimes we do it because we don't know what else to do.

Only by moving to the present will we be able to take control of our lives and cope with our family's pain. Separation, loss, and grief are normal; they are common. Our situation is unique as to its particulars, but not its category. All of us suffer loss, and there may be no clear answer to "why?"

A gentleman who suffered enormous physical pain was asked why this happened to him. "Why not me?" he replied. Why shouldn't injuries, diseases, loss, and pain come to us? Is there some reason why God or destiny or fortune or any other force should have made us exempt from tragedy? Separation sooner or later is everyone's normal lot. Unfortunately, the separation from young people often comes too soon.

Searching for Purpose

Attempting to find meaning and purpose in the events surrounding our broken hearts is a valid goal. Life needs meaning and purpose. The mistake many of us make is looking for purpose in the tragedy itself. Real meaning is found only in our *response* to that tragedy.

A 15-year-old boy is killed in a car accident. What is the purpose in that son's death? There is none. We shouldn't try to force some magic accomplishment into the death itself.

Some people may say the boy died because God was lonely and needed more angels or that God wanted to teach the lad a lesson. Others speculate that God punished the boy or that God knew what kind of hard life he was going to lead and removed him early. None of these answers is satisfactory.

121

When a teen is delinquent, some may say that God is teaching us patience or preparing us for a rough future. Others may say God is testing our faith—as if God would turn the son into a bank robber so we would recognize our frailty. None of these answers is satisfactory either.

Purpose can be found in the tragedy that comes through our children. The purpose is found in how we handle those events. Pain, agony, heartbreak, disaster, and loss have no meaning in themselves. Meaning is discovered by our response to those terrible events.

If a daughter becomes addicted to drugs, the addiction serves no purpose. It was not good that she used drugs or wrecked her mind and body. That was bad. However, if her awful experience causes us to express our love more, to grow closer to her siblings, or to volunteer at a youth center, purpose has come out of the tragedy.

Many parents facing painful disappointment eventually look for solace in a well-known passage of Scripture, Romans 8:28: "And we know that in all things God works for the good of those who love him, who have been called according to his purpose." Understood correctly this verse addresses our dilemma.

The verse does not assure the reader that all things are good. Some things are lousy, bad, and terrible. Paul, the author, is not simply trying to put the best light on everything, nor is he using hollow words in an attempt to comfort those who are grieving.

When bad things happen in our families, God is willing to work those events into something that will be good. God wants to draw gain out of the pain. If we cooperate with God to find the good, we turn the terrible situation into something that has purpose and meaning.

On the other hand, if we throw up our hands and curse the suffering, we intensify the loss. Spirituality can help us turn bad into good. That is God's offer in Romans 8:28.

We cannot expect God to change the past. We do not ask God to tell us that alcoholism, death, or estrangement were really good, but merely disguised. We will not ask God to help us rejoice in our child's arrest. Rather, we ask God to help us look for ways to turn the tragedy into some valuable meaning in the future. Only then do we make sense out of the verse and put it to maximum use and relief.

On December 12, 1994, Teresa McGovern died on the snow-covered ground in Madison, Wisconsin. Forty-five years old, she lost her battle with alcoholism and died of exposure. Her father, George McGovern, former U.S. Senator and democratic nominee for president in 1972, spoke freely of his love for her as "a special joy to our family." As an adult, Teresa brought joy to many of her friends and, according to her father, also allowed them to share part of her suffering.

As I read McGovern's article, I could sense a brokenhearted father trying to give meaning to his daughter's tragedy. Maybe by speaking out he thought he could help other families with sons and daughters in similar situations.

Loss has meaning if we reach out to touch others, if we permit ourselves the strength to grow, or if we find new ways to express love, faith, and caring.

The Compassionate Friends organization is a prime example. The group consists of parents who have lost a child in death. Its members have bound themselves together to help other parents who have also lost a child. They provide support for parents by newsletters, lending libraries, speakers, support groups, and telephone friends.

Something good has come out of something terrible. That isn't why the terrible thing happened. But it does provide an opportunity to rise up and see something good come from it.

Giving Ourselves Time

Not everyone is ready for this message. Some of us remain fixed on the loss for a long time. A mother might spend ten years concentrating on her defiant daughter's deviant lifestyle. Every day she might torture herself over the child's failure to turn around. That parent isn't ready. She continues to drown in her misery. If a life preserver is thrown to her, she will choose to reject it.

For more than five years a man in Louisville has made daily trips to visit the grave of his teenage son. This father isn't ready. He doesn't want to hear about meaning, purpose, love, or today. In a way, his life ended when his son's car crossed over the yellow line. He isn't ready to go on.

Moving on to purpose demands a conscious decision. No one is capable of removing our grief if we choose to fixate on the loss.

For some parents all they have left of their rebellious, defiant child is the grief that accompanied his actions. The young man shows no sign of changing his attitude and treating his parents in a civil, loving way. The parents feel the only part of their son they can successfully hold onto is the rebellious side. If someone tells them to move on, the parents believe the final thread of relationship is threatened. They believe if they give up their grief, they will have nothing left of their son.

Each of us must decide when it is time to move on. We have to accept the fact that looking for the good will neither desecrate the memory of our child, nor erase any contact with him. Moving on only adds meaning to other relationships.

The message isn't, "Forget your child and get on with life." The better message is, "Accept the pain for what it is and rise up to make something good happen."

Not all parents are public speakers, group leaders, or writers, but they don't need to be. Purpose might be found in the new way they treat their other children. Meaning could be expressed in their relationship with the grandchildren. The good could be realized in the parents' renewed love for each other.

No one should try to limit the good God will be able to work out with our cooperation and dedication. There must be as many ways to carry out meaning as there are stars in the sky.

Willingness and awareness are the key attitudes. We must not permit pain to drive us into retreat. We must determine, by God's grace, to turn our energies around and lead the charge back into life.

Pain and loss are not the biggest waste. But pain and loss that don't result in some form of good are indeed total emptiness.

None of us should be surprised, however, if it takes a while before we can begin to turn our loss into meaning. It takes time to accept our loss. It takes time to adjust to the sad facts. We have been wounded. Those wounds will need time and help to heal. Only as the healing takes place will we be able to identify the good we might create.

We don't walk out of the jail, the hospital, or the mortuary and look for a new mission. The hurt might be too great to imagine we would want to trust or get involved again. But with the healing will come new energy and new direction, and we will feel far more like pursuing it.

Chapter 20

Children of Adoption

Don't be surprised at the stories you hear about adoption. As with other families, some turn into positive situations while others crash and burn. Since adoptive families are made up of flesh, blood, psychological, and spiritual people, we have no right to expect anything else.

One child will rise up to be a missionary; another will spend years behind bars. This is part of the human dynamic and nothing can be guaranteed otherwise. Many parents expected otherwise because they meant well. They did a good deed by adopting, they prayed carefully over the decision, they loved the child with dedication, and they were there whenever he or she needed them. But with all their best intentions, life took a bad turn. That's part of the human condition.

Ask Joseph, the "father" of Jesus. His family also was a non-genetic family. Joseph didn't know what to expect. The very thought of the prospect left him speechless. Eventually he accepted the heavenly message (Matt. 1:20-24), but it wasn't easy.

As time went by Joseph would still have to wrestle with the bewilderment of it all. Not perfect people and not a perfect family, Joseph and Mary took everything as it came and did what they could without a handbook. Mostly, they must have felt good that they tried.

Not a Complete Family

Speaking at a symposium, a gentleman who had worked for 20 years with adoptive families concluded that two families never become one. Think that over. You may wish that wasn't true, but it probably is. Everyone in the family could be perfectly fine. Each member might love the other without reservation. But so many other factors are at work that a total fit is almost too much to ask. In my years as a licensed counselor I have learned a great deal about adoptions, but I realize that a short book like this cannot totally do justice to the subject.

Most adoptees will always wonder about their original families. What were they like? Why did their parent(s) give them up? Did they have a choice? Have they been told the truth? Should the children try to find their birth parents?

We have no way of knowing what the child is wondering unless he tells us. If given the opportunity, will he tell us? We have no right to insist that he do so. There is a chamber inside the child where we might never be able to travel. We can furnish opportunities, but we cannot try to tear down doors.

The adoptive families I have known have tried to be accessible. When the child is ready to discuss his or her family of origin, the adoptive parents are willing to talk. They also want to tell the truth. At other times, the parents may need to guide the child in certain directions. It may not be enough to wait to see what the child might want to know. Some things about alcohol, drugs, abuse, and disease he eventually must know.

To Love and Be Loved

Adoptive parents who are waiting to be loved are making a painful mistake. Parents who adopt love the child. But if their goal is to get the child to love them, they are likely to fail. The same is true of biological parents. "Why don't you love me?" is an unworthy question. We must love the child unconditionally.

Our love should not depend on their love either. We dare not love only the children who love us. They may not be mature enough to play that game. Our responsibility is to love them anyway.

Unworthy Questions

All of us occasionally are hung up on the fence when we ask questions that cannot help. A few of these may be:

- **Should I have adopted?** You did. Now let's move on to reality.
- **Should I have asked more questions?** Don't dabble in the past. Get into the present. Go to the agency and ask them whatever you still don't understand.
- **Does the child have psychological problems?** Be specific. Visit a counselor and explain your concerns. The problems may have little to do with adoption.
- **Should I go easier on him because he is adopted?** Everyone needs discipline. Feeling sorry for the child won't help.
- **I was harsh with him at first. How do I make up for that?** You don't. Deal with today. Otherwise, it all becomes entangled.
- **Why did this happen to me?** There are many answers to this question, and they are probably all wrong. The only important and helpful questions at this point begin with, "What now?"

Worthy Questions

- **How do I accept myself?** You have good intentions. Congratulate yourself on all the ways you have helped.
- **Am I a valuable person?** The Bible is filled with stories of parents who worked hard and yet their child chose

another way. You did all right. You can't control all of the results.
- **What things did I do okay?** Without *dwelling* on the past, take time to add up the positive things you did. To say you didn't do anything right is to deny reality, which never helps.
- **Were we the best parents ever? Were we the worst parents ever?** Neither one.
- **When will we stop parenting?** Rise up now and become a friend to the adult child. Parenting a 36-year-old child does not work.

Meaning in Suffering

How many adoptive parents do you know? Invite them to your home and share your feelings. With whom are you angry? With whom are you happy? Slowly share those feelings with others and listen carefully to what they say.

There is no need to trash your child in front of others, but it could be healthy to release some pent-up tensions. As we talk and listen, genuine healing becomes a real possibility.

Closure is improbable. Though it is a popular buzz word right now, some dilemmas never go away. Some parents have not reached closure with their adopted child and never will. Situations often become better, but frequently they do not.

We might teach a Sunday School class and dedicate our effort to the child whom we can no longer reach. We might write an anonymous article on what we have learned. A short-term support group could enable several parents help each other.

Busyness by itself is not likely to fill many voids. However, meaningful activity could help chase away some of the ache.

Releasing the Bio-Parents

When life hurts, we are tempted to curse others. If we have bad feelings toward the biological parents, our disdain for them will only intensify. Beware. Any growing blame against the parents of origin, living or dead, can only exacerbate our problems. There is still no way for parents to change history. Blame is likely to turn into hate, and hate is cancerous in nature. Forgiving the bio-parents may not be the issue. However, we must move on. Moving backward only digs deeper holes. We raise children to release them. Often, we cannot reach the plateau we had hoped. This is common. However, it would be a mistake to try to recreate our past.

Thank God for the opportunity to introduce love to a child's life. Our challenges now must be centered on the present and the future. God continues to be good.

Chapter 21

Eating Pudding Pies

Before learning he was diabetic, a friend enjoyed apple pie. When his medical problem was discovered, however, he had to give up those delicious pies. At first he complained and felt sorry for himself, but as time went by, he discovered sugar-free pudding pies. Granted, they weren't apple pies, but after a while the adjustment went fairly well.

Today my friend knows he will probably never be able to eat regular apple pies, and he still misses them. But he has decided to lick his lips and enjoy pudding pies as if they were delicacies from the finest ovens.

Similarly, tomorrow will be different for each broken-hearted parent. A few will never see their child again. Others will be reunited with bonds that are stronger than ever. Most of us will be somewhere in the middle with a mixture of highs and lows, of enthusiasm and pain.

Most of us will learn to eat the pie that is set before us. We will enjoy what we can have and stop cursing what we cannot have. Frustrated, hurt, and disappointed, we will now decide to go on and accept all the good gifts that God sends our way. We will enjoy whatever family relationship we can pull together. We will be glad to reach out and participate even on a limited scale.

And by the grace of God, we will make the most of anything we can have.

Life will go on. We will meet new people, help those who need us, and develop new relationships. We will praise God, serve Him, and ask for more wisdom.

Out of serious setback and genuine pain, we will rise up to grasp each day. And the day will bring us new satisfaction because we have decided to reach for all it has to offer.

Sharing with Others

With most tragedies, we find the strength to go on by sharing our experiences with others in need. Millions of parents have had their hearts broken. The majority keep the story to themselves and never receive help. If more would open up to tell others their experience, many other parents could have their burdens lifted dramatically.

This isn't an easy subject to discuss. It isn't like fly-fishing, baseball, or handcraft. There are risks involved and agonies to relive. We can understand anyone's reluctance to hang it out on the clothesline of life.

But healing comes by sharing. It also comes by listening. Whenever two people can share and listen, they have the full potential of rising above their wounds. Find an avenue to express your pain. By expressing it, the sharpness will diminish for both the speaker and the hearer.

Finding Spiritual Strength

The Old Testament prophets looked for a Messiah who would eventually come and "bind up the brokenhearted" (Isaiah 61:1). Jesus told us this passage of Scripture has now been fulfilled (Luke 4:16-21). To this day, aiding the brokenhearted remains a major part of the ongoing ministry of Jesus Christ.

His invitation, "Come unto me, all ye that labour and are heavy laden and I will give you rest" (Matthew 11:28,

KJV), includes parents who suffer within their own families. Increasingly, we acknowledge our need for spiritual strength as we plow our way through life. That spiritual strength can be found by depending on Christ and the Holy Spirit in terribly trying times.

Spirituality will give us a sense of belonging, a feeling of outside power, a forgiving spirit, a wider perspective, an attitude of tolerance, and purpose in life. It will provide someone to talk to, quiet moments of guidance, courage to rise above circumstances, a knowledge that someone larger than us actually cares, and much more. Spiritual strength is more than a slogan, and many professional caregivers have come to accept that reality.

True spirituality teaches that if apple pie is taken away from us, we should go after pudding pie as if it were a delicacy. We must concentrate on what we have, instead of brooding over what we do not have.

Thankfulness helps us rise up to take on the day with all of its challenges, gifts, and goodness. We can thank God for every ray of sunshine that comes our way.

look at your own
deflections –

– watch what you *do*,

expecting to Lord

how to let
response –